Parent Power

Parent Power

ENERGIZING HOME-SCHOOL COMMUNICATION

Brenda Power

with

Mary Bagley

Anna Brown

Kelly Chandler

Kerri Doyle

Nathan Merrill

Susan Rossignol

Field Consultant: Gail Gibson

Heinemann

PORTSMOUTH, NH

HEINEMANN
A division of Reed Elsevier Inc.
361 Hanover Street
Portsmouth, NH 03801-3912
http://www.heinemann.com

Offices and agents throughout the world

Library of Congress Cataloging-in-Publication Data

CIP is on file with the Library of Congress.

ISBN 0-325-00155-3

Editor: Lois Bridges
Production: Melissa L. Inglis
Cover design: Catherine Hawkes/Cat and Mouse Design
Manufacturing: Louise Richardson

Printed in the United States of America on acid-free paper
03 02 01 00 99   ML   1 2 3 4 5

Special thanks to

the Mapleton, Maine, Elementary School Staff

About the *Parent Power* CD-ROM

The *Parent Power* CD contains a variety of resources that will allow you to make full use of the information and essays contained in this resource guide. The CD will work in both Macintosh and Windows systems. To explore the CD, just place the disc in the CD drive of your computer. Double-click on the CD icon once it is displayed on screen and the contents of the CD will be displayed.

- The "Read Me" file repeats the information on this page to allow you a quick reference to the CD contents.

- The "Essays.pdf" file provides an exact copy of every essay contained in *Parent Power*. The essays in this file are formatted just as they appear in this book. You can use this file as a backup in case the essays in the book become damaged in any way. The "Essays.pdf" file also provides an index of the essays and allows you to search the essay text for particular words or ideas. The file is readable only using the software Adobe Acrobat Reader, which is provided on the CD. To install Acrobat Reader on your machine, simply double-click on the Acrobat folder on the CD and then run the enclosed installation program.

- The "Essay Text Files" folder contains the unformatted text of the essays (both English and Spanish versions) in ASCII format. This file format allows you to import the essays into any word processing or layout program so you can customize the text to suit your needs. For example, you can personalize the essays to reflect particular events in your classroom, or import them into a school newsletter or brochure. The file names in the "Essay Text Files" folder follow the essay names here in the book. Specifically, the file names combine the essay number and several beginning words from the title of the essay.

- The "Getting Started" file launches a demonstration of the many ways you can use the information on the CD. It shows how to search the essays in the PDF file ("Essays.pdf") and how to print the essays from the disc. It also shows how to open the text files using a word processing or layout program. Finally, the Getting Started demonstration contains numerous examples of ways to customize the essays to suit the needs of your school community. To run the Getting Started demonstration, simply double-click on the "Getting Started" icon.

A Reminder About Licenses

When you purchased *Parent Power,* you purchased either a Single User License or a Multiple User License. The rights associated with each of these licenses are described below.

- *Single User License.* This license permits use of the book and CD (including photocopying and customizing the essays) by an individual teacher for the purpose of communicating with the families of the children in his or her classroom. This license is also appropriate when purchase of *Parent Power* is required as part of a university course. It is not intended for use by a whole school or in a library setting.

- *Multiple User License.* This license permits use of the book and CD (including photocopying and customizing the essays) by all members of a school community. It is appropriate both for use in a library setting where everyone in the school building will be able to read and use the essays and for use as part of a whole-school communication. It is also appropriate when *Parent Power* will be used as a reference for all students in a university course.

CONTENTS

LIST of FIGURES

Part 1

Teacher's Guide

Chapter 1

INTRODUCTION

Every day when my young daughter bounds off the school bus, I get her a snack and we chat about her school day. After we talk, I always pounce on the blue folder in her backpack that contains correspondence from her teacher. It might be a personal note about a class project, or a letter sent to all parents about events from the week. But whatever the writing from the teacher, I marvel at how it always feels "just right"—packed with information, good humor, and a respect for parents as partners in their children's education.

As teachers, we all want those "just right" communications with parents. Depending upon the needs of the parents and children we work with, that communication can take many forms—from notes and fact sheets to newsletters and evening workshops.

The essays and advice in this resource guide are tools to help you find new ways to communicate and work with parents. They are designed to be used with parents of children in the primary grades (K–3). While all parents at all grade levels want to be involved in their children's education, K–3 parents often have the greatest need for information since school is a relatively new phenomenon in their child's life.

For the parent who is not able to go to school functions, these essays can be read in the quick moments when a book bag or lunch box is being cleaned out. They are not designed to advocate for certain styles of teaching, and any complex terminology has been omitted in explaining best practices in learning and parenting. Written in basic, jargon-free language, these essays can supplement an existing parent communication program, or they can serve as a foundation for beginning a new one.

The materials in this guide build—from the simple one- or two-page essays that can be sent home to educate parents, to strategies for designing comprehensive community outreach programs. Find your own starting point, based upon your experience working with parents and the needs of your students and school. This guide can help any teacher or school get started with a parent outreach program. Many suggestions involve investing only a few minutes a week in getting organized and sending home materials.

You may also have a focused area of need in your parent outreach program. For example, if you already schedule many creative events for parents but wonder how to get more attention in the community, the sections on connecting with the media (pages 34–37) will probably be the most helpful to you.

For readers who want to design a home-school communication plan, this resource guide is chock-full of tips from teachers for working with parents in dynamic ways. These strategies will help you learn how to manage your time and resources better so that parent involvement can be naturally integrated into your school routine.

Chapter 2

USING THE ESSAYS IN A PARENT OUTREACH PROGRAM

The essays in this guide are divided into two categories:

1. curriculum/school concerns
2. general parenting issues

You might want to skim quickly through the essays in Part 2, beginning on page 43, to get a sense of their tone and style. The curriculum essays explain appropriate strategies for collaborating with teachers and how school learning can be supported at home. The general parenting essays (e.g., on limiting television, coping with childhood stress) can help parents learn new techniques and principles for improving the home environment to support learning at school.

Regardless of how extensive or simple you decide your home-school communication program will be, you may want to:

- *Choose a distinctive color for all your important home-school communication.* If you let parents know at the start of the year that all newsletters and important forms will be on mint green or cherry pink paper, this material will be less likely to get lost. Families will learn to look for the color and pull it out of piles of work that goes home.
- *Pick one weekday for sending home key home-school communication, and try to stick with it.* Early in the week seems to work better—materials that require a response and go home on Thursday or Friday are more likely to be lost over the weekend. Many teachers choose to put newsletters, announcements, and materials that need to be returned in brightly colored manila envelopes that go home on Monday or Tuesday, to be returned within twenty-four hours. This regular routine assures parents that they won't be missing important news, and the quick turnaround helps teachers keep track of permission slips, volunteer rosters, and other forms.

Figure 1 is a sample calendar of when the essays might be sent home, linked to school events. There is no one right way for using these essays to communicate with parents—how you distribute them will depend upon the goals you set for your parent communication program.

The essays are far more likely to be read by parents if they include a personal note from the teacher or school. These notes can announce special events or highlight some aspect of the curriculum from the learning during the week. For example, the essay on parent-teacher conferences can be attached to a form for signing up for conferences in October. The essay on "Everyday Math" can be used to announce the completion of a big math project and remind parents of a special family math event (see Figure 2).

Another possibility for using the essays is to copy a general essay for parents on one side and then write a specific letter or note for parents on the other. Parents will come to expect and enjoy these notes from you. They needn't be long or detailed—any short and friendly update will help parents feel more connected to what is going on in the classroom.

For example, Jill Ostrow finds that students in her grades 1–3 multiage classroom are always very tired during the early days of the

AUGUST		
Week	*Parent Essay Number and Topic*	**Announcements/Notes**
Week 1 (before school starts)	5: Helping Your Child Enter a New School	Announce "First Day of School" Celebration; invite parents to volunteer orientation session early September.
SEPTEMBER		
Week 1	3: Adjusting to School	Send home parent survey.
Week 2	13: Getting Involved in Your Child's Classroom	Update parents on volunteer offers from survey so far; send home survey again for those who haven't completed it.
Week 3	18: Using the Library with Your Child	Announce library hours; send with take-home manila folder packs—each containing children's book, parent/child reading log, and instructions.
Week 4	6: Television and Learning	Announce three good age-appropriate shows/times for viewing during the week. Could also include information about when/if you plan to use video materials during the year.
OCTOBER		
Week 1	21: Meeting with Your Child's Teacher, Part 1: Preparation	Announce Parent Conferences.
Week 2	22: Meeting with Your Child's Teacher, Part 2: The Main Event	
Week 3	27: Everyday Math	Announce Family Math Night.
Week 4	28: Math at Home	
Week 5	4: Dealing with Concerns	
NOVEMBER		
Week 1	35: "Big Ideas" in Science	Announce Family Science Night.
Week 2	23: Nutrition: Raising Low-Fat Kids	Announce "Healthy Kids" Cooking Demonstration; ask for recipe contributions to "Healthy Kids" parent association cookbook fundraiser.
Week 3	20: Reading with Your Child	
Week 4	19: Talking with Your Child About School	
DECEMBER		
Week 1	9: Coping with Conflict	Announce "Sibling Rivalry" Workshop for Parents.
Week 2	11: Children's Hobbies	
Week 3	7: To View or Not to View: Evaluating Television Programs	
Week 4	No newsletter: vacation week	

Figure 1   *Sample Calendar for Distributing Essays*

JANUARY		
Week	Parent Essay Number and Topic	Announcements/Notes
Week 1	25: Homework, Part 1: Setting the Stage	
Week 2	26: Homework, Part 2: Coaching Your Child	
Week 3	14: Reading Around the House	Announce Four-Part Reading Workshop for Parent Volunteer Mentors.
Week 4	12: Understanding Phonics	
Week 5	37: A Love of Music	Announce Family Band and Orchestra Night.

FEBRUARY		
Week 1	30: We Know What You Want...	
Week 2	1: Writing at Home	Announce Family Writing Night.
Week 3	No newsletter: vacation week	
Week 4	2: Asking About Groups	

MARCH		
Week 1	8: Appreciating Art—Child Style	Announce Community Arts Festival.
Week 2	33: Best Web Sites for Parents	Announce "Getting Tight with Technology" Night.
Week 3	31: Daily To-Do List	
Week 4	36: Childhood Friends	Announce School Spring Cleanup.

APRIL		
Week 1	15: Alternatives to Grades	
Week 2	29: Displaying and Storing Children's Work	Announce School Rummage Sale.
Week 3	No newsletter: vacation week	
Week 4	40: Telling Family Tales	Announce Cultural Cookout.

MAY		
Week 1	39: Spelling	Announce Author's Fair.
Week 2	16: Standardized Tests, Part 1	
Week 3	17: Standardized Tests, Part 2	
Week 4	10: Building a Low-Cost Library of Books	Announce "Leap into Summer" Book Exchange.
Week 5	24: The Power of a Map	

JUNE		
Week 1	32: Praise and Self-Esteem	
Week 2	38: On Vacation...But Not from Learning!	Announce July Concert in the Park/School Picnic.

Essay 34 "Meeting with a Specialist" was not used in a newletter—it was sent home with individual children with requests for meetings between parents, teachers, and specialists.

Figure 1   *Sample Calendar for Distributing Essays, continued*

year. Her letter to parents about student fatigue during the first week of school is warm, funny, and reassuring. It could easily be used on one side of the page, with the other side filled by the essay in this guide on adjusting to school (see Figures 3A and 3B).

Some of the essays in Part 2 might be best used to highlight special events, activities, or whole-school goals. In Figure 4, the essay "Using the Library with Your Child" was reformatted for use in a folded brochure. This brochure enables parents to get library cards for the family and announces special events at the town library planned all year long.

Everyday Math

So what does a bologna sandwich in a lunch box have to do with learning math? Everything—in classrooms where everyday experiences with math problems are valued. Your child might be asked to survey classmates to discover what they have packed in their lunch boxes, and then to chart the results on a graph. Comparing the number of bologna sandwiches to peanut butter sandwiches to hot lunch purchases leads children into concepts of numbers, percentages, and visually representing information.

Students need to see everyday uses of math for solving simple and complex problems. Children still learn the math facts and concepts that were valued when you were a student—but they are often learning them in different ways. Here are some newer practices in math that are used to help children see math as a natural, everyday process.

- *Open-Ended Problems.* Children are being given more math problems that don't have a clear "right" answer. No one knows how many children prefer cats to dogs as pets when that survey question is asked and charted, or what the ratio is of the size of a child's hand to the length of a desktop before it is measured.
- *Hands-on, Minds-on Activities.* You'll notice that your child is doing many more math activities beyond practicing adding, subtracting, or fractions on worksheets. Students are being pushed to find more than one route to get to an answer. What this promotes in children is a willingness to try more than once in tackling a problem, building their ability to see more complex problems later in more sophisticated ways.
- *Math Journals/Learning Logs.* As children try out many possible solutions, they are challenged to write about their process in math so they can become more aware of the steps they take to get to an answer.

As your child develops mathematical skills, teachers and parents can work together to ensure that math is more than getting the right answer (though in the end that's important too!). Becoming a strong mathematician involves seeing more and more possibilities for using numbers to solve complicated problems, and using numbers as a tool to understand the world. Encourage your child to play with math, and notice the everyday math in tasks you do every day.

[Handwritten:] We're finishing our math unit on surveys and graphs this week. Don't forget to mark your calendar for our school's Family Math Night on Wednesday, October 14th from 7:00–8:30 P.M. Bring the whole family—everyone is welcome!

Figure 2   *Essay Example Linked to School Event*

Dear Parents:

If you are the parent of a first-grade child, you may have noticed them coming home tired and cranky from school. No, I am not torturing them! Being tired and cranky is perfectly **NORMAL** for the first three months of school. *Really.* Some children take three entire months to fully adjust to school. If you don't believe me, ask some of the parents who have older children in the room. Your child may even be irritable and say that they don't want to come back to school—that they hate school. This is also normal. I've been at school for these first two days, and believe me, no one is miserable!

Seriously, I've been teaching for years and this is the only aspect about child development that is *always* consistent. It may not be pleasant for you when they come home, but they're all doing great in class! Also, don't expect your child to explain very much about their day. It's a bit overwhelming at first in our room as a lot happens during the day; it's hard to remember (especially when you're tired).

The kids have already worked in groups and partnerships and it's only Day 2! The more experienced members of the community are really helping the new members. They are helping the new members learn about respect and tolerance. Respect is key in our room, and it's the experienced children who teach this to the new children.

Anyway, we're having a great first few days. Don't forget snacks! It's a long morning.

Jill Ostrow

Figure 3A   *Side One of Letter to Parents (First Week of School)*

Adjusting to School

You may notice that the house is a little quiet the first week of school! This is only natural as everyone adjusts to the new routines of schools. Don't expect most children to be very chatty—it's exhausting for anyone to juggle new classrooms, friends, early bedtimes, and earlier wake-up calls! It is an exciting but bewildering time for children—new friends, new teachers, and new responsibilities can overwhelm even the most confident child. There are small things you can do that your child will appreciate to help them adjust to the new school year:

- *Make sure home routines are very regular.* This provides children with a sense of security as they adjust to the new demands of school. Firm bedtimes and consistent routines such as reading together just before lights out will help your child master the new routines away from home much more quickly.

- *Organize that book bag!* Now is the time for you to set up a quiet area, time, and ground rules for help with school projects or homework. Read any materials sent home about the school rules and routines carefully, so you can help your child with new responsibilities and rules.

- *Hide a note or two.* Write a short note to your children reminding them that you're thinking of them all day long, and then hide it in their lunch or backpack. Your child will love coming across a happy note from home as they are in the midst of adjusting to a new environment.

- *Plan a special event for the weekend.* It might include preparing your child's favorite meal, or a last trip to the beach or favorite playground. Celebrate the hard work your child (and you) have done all week adjusting to school by treating yourselves to time together you can both enjoy.

Figure 3B   *Side Two of Letter*

Using the Evergreen Town Library with Your Child

A Guide for Evergreen School Families

2000–2001 School Year

Using the Library with Your Child

Your local library is a resource within your community that not only builds knowledge but also builds a lifelong love of reading. The library can become a comfortable place for you and your child to share good times together.

- **Make library time a special time.**
  Let your child get their very own library card. This gives your child a sense of importance and responsibility for their own reading education. You should also have your own library card. When you bring your child to the library, stay and enjoy the library yourself. While your child is browsing for books, find books for yourself. You can select books that you want to share with your child or adult books that you want to read on your own. Make library time a regular part of your schedule, preferably once a week. This gives your child something to look forward to each week.

- **Enjoy other library resources.**
  There are a variety of resources for you and your child at your local library. Libraries have thousands of wonderful books for you to borrow and enjoy. However, books are not the only materials offered to you from your library. Most libraries have a section that offers current and back issues of the most popular magazines and newspapers. In addition to reading materials, most libraries offer videos, music, and books on cassette.

- **Go to special events.**
  There are a variety of activities and programs available. Most public libraries have a special time for children called "Story Hour." At this time your child is read to by an experienced storyteller. Many times these sessions include drama and question-and-answer periods. Some other activities that may be offered at your library are puppet shows, guest speakers, movies, arts and crafts, and reading programs. Call your local library to get a schedule of upcoming events.

Evergreen Town Library Card Application

By special arrangement with the Evergreen Town Library, we've arranged for family registrations for library cards through the school. If you don't have a town library card yet, simply fill out the form below and have your child bring it back to school.

Names of Family Members

1 _____ Age _____
2 _____ Age _____
3 _____ Age _____
4 _____ Age _____
5 _____ Age _____
6 _____ Age _____

Mailing Address:
Street _____ Town/Zip Code _____
Phone Number _____

clip and save clip and save clip and save clip and save

Special Events at the Evergreen Town Library for Evergreen School Families

November 7 and November 14 7–8 P.M.
Storytelling Workshops for Parents
(childcare provided)

March 13 7 P.M.
Readathon Award Winners Announced with Readings
by Local Authors

April 28 5–9 P.M.
"Artravanganza" Festival

June 15 6:30–8 P.M.
Leap into Summer Book Exchange

Watch for more information on each of these events
in the school newsletter.

Figure 4   *Sample Brochure*

Chapter 3

TIPS FOR DESIGNING NEWSLETTERS

Newsletters are like bulletin boards—they can trumpet some of the liveliest work of the year for a larger audience...and they can also become the bane of a teacher's existence. But like bulletin boards, newsletters are worth the time and effort it takes to create them. Brief, well-designed newsletters will be read by parents—there are few better vehicles for getting their attention. The good news is that there are many time-savers available to help teachers create newsletters in a fraction of the time it took in years past.

Here are some simple strategies for moving from using the essays as stand-alone flyers to integrating them into newsletters.

Divide and Conquer

Consider writing a joint newsletter with other teachers at your grade level, or if your school is small, with the whole staff. Figure out what each teacher's strengths are, and divvy up the jobs accordingly. If at least one teacher on your staff is a computer whiz, she or he can be responsible for formatting. Another teacher can compile the events of the week; still another can ferret out good quotes about teaching, parenting, and kids from newspapers and magazines.* If one teacher is assigned the most challenging task of writing up feature articles,

---

*Very short quotes from other sources can be quoted in classroom newsletters as long as the source is referenced. However, for longer quotes, permission from the publisher is necessary. You should check with your school legal counsel for further guidance.

consider bartering to free up time to accomplish this. Newsletter writing time might be exchanged for lunch or recess duties during the week.

Use Existing Desktop Publishing Programs

Figure 5 is an example of a school newsletter using the newsletter templates from Clarisworks. Essays from this guide can be integrated into other announcements of school and classroom events in the newsletters. Almost all major word-processing programs include a newsletter template similar to these.

Create Standard Features

Decide individually or with your colleagues what features you want to have in every newsletter. Some possible features to consider:

- a round-up of activities in each classroom
- announcements of school events
- an essay from this resource guide
- very quick summaries of recent research or facts related to schooling and parenting
- a "question of the week" for families
- an "activity of the week" for parents to complete with children
- a fun cartoon or clipart
- a weekly message from a "special guest" (varying from week to week, these guests could include custodial staff, administrators, lunch workers, bus drivers, school volunteers)

The Family Connection

Edited by Ms. Richards and the Second Graders in Room 114   October 12, 2001

notes from Ms. Richards

This week we continued our environmental study of local plants, in preparation for next week's visit to the Hillside Apple Orchard. Attached is the field trip form. If you've lost your master calendar of all parent/community activities for the year, don't worry! We'll be sending home additional copies next week. And if you have saved your copy, just pass the new calendar on to grandparents or other family members in the community.

Guest Speaker a Hit

Our thanks to Linda Campbell's dad, who provided a demonstration of edible herbs after leading a nature walk in the school woods as part of our "Be Good to the Environment" unit. The children pronounced them umm umm good. Everyone was fascinated by the presentation.

quotable quote:

Everyone needs a child to teach. That's the way adults learn.

Author Unknown

upcoming special events:

November 1st   10 a.m.
Grandparent Visit: Felice Constanza

Mrs. Constanza is Theresa Goodson's grandmother. She was born in Mexico, and moved to the United States almost forty years ago. She will share stories from her life, in preparation for our "Family Stories and Traditions" unit that we will undertake throughout the upcoming holiday season. We'll have more on how you can connect this unit with storytelling at home in our next newsletter.

November 8th   7 p.m.
Family Science Night
Sponsored by the Evergreen Third Grade

The third-grade class has lots of fun planned for the whole family, including adventures with "oobleck." Wear comfortable clothes, and expect the whole family to enjoy the science experiments and "fun facts" from science available in every classroom. If you want to prepare for the night ahead of time, you might want to read Dr. Seuss's OOBLECK, available from our class library or at the Evergreen Town Library.

Feature Topic: Writing at Home

Imagine trying to learn to ride a bike without ever falling off or learning to play the piano without ever hitting a wrong note. It can't be done—learning to do anything well involves taking risks and making mistakes. Learning to write is also a process of trial and error in schools and at home. Practice is what helps anyone learn a new skill, with a little gentle guidance from someone who has already mastered that skill. There are things you can do as a parent to help your child enjoy this time of learning to write:

• Keep paper, pencils, markers, and crayons around. Ask your children what kind of materials they like to write with, and then set up a small storage area that includes some writing supplies.

• Remember that "writing" is drawing for many young learners. Children will make pictures before they write words. Ask you children to explain what they've drawn to you—the explanation often is a story that is the germ of an idea for writing. And make sure to do a little writing and drawing with your children—you will be amazed at the conversations that take place while you are sketching and writing together.

• Treat your children with new writing tools. For a special surprise, buy some nice writing paper on sale, or scented markers you know your children will enjoy. New tools can spark new interest in writing.

• Let your children help you write. Whenever you're writing down a phone message, grocery list, or note, ask your children if they would like to write with you. Let them write their own version, side by side with you.

• Don't worry about correctness too early. Remember that the attempt is what matters with children—if they see you celebrate seeing them put pen to paper, they will want to write more. Children can easily be overwhelmed by too much advice and criticism, no matter how gently it is given.

we can't forget:

• To thank the many family members who showed up for "Family Math Night" last week.

• To remind everyone that we are the sponsoring class for the Artravanganza Art Festival at Evergreen Town Library in April. Our parent volunteer coordinator, Lynn Russell, will be sending home more information in next week's newsletter.

• To encourage everyone to sign out materials from our parent resource library. Books linked to this week's feature story include:

WRITE FROM THE START by Donald Graves and Virginia Stuart

WRITING BEGINS AT HOME by Marie Clay

FAMILIES WRITING by Peter Stillman

Figure 5   *Sample Newsletter*

Less Is More

It's better to send home a two-page newsletter consistently, on the same day of the week or month, than to have a larger newsletter that varies wildly in quality or is produced on a haphazard schedule. Parents (particularly those who are not avid readers) are much more likely to read something that is short and information-packed than they are to wade through pages of extra features and examples of student work.

Use the Web for Information

There are a number of Web sites that have many materials that might be used in newsletters for parents (see Figure 6 on page 14). These can be bookmarked and referred to when you're struggling to fill your newsletter. You might also list some of them in a newsletter for parents who are especially computer-savvy. If you do provide this information for parents, make sure you include information about when libraries and school computer labs are available for use by parents who don't have Internet access in their homes.

Purchase Some Materials to Use in Newsletters

Purchasing some clipart and graphic materials can add pizzazz to your newsletters at a small cost to your school. There are a number of both hard and electronic clipart collections available with a school focus—many multipurpose word-processing programs include at least a small amount of school-related clipart.

Enlist Parent or Student Volunteers to Help

Some parents who can't volunteer during the day might be able to do the desktop publishing, writing, or layout for your newsletter on a regular basis. These tasks are easy for someone who is computer literate, and there is some flexibility about when the work needs to be completed. If you put out a call for assistance late in the summer, you might be surprised at the expertise available.

Students in upper-grade classes who are computer literate also might be able to assist with the newsletter. Ask your colleagues who teach in the upper grades or work at the high school computer lab if they know any conscientious students who might enjoy the work.

Sites for Parents

Parent Soup and The Family Education Network are two of the largest professionally run Web sites for parents. Parent Soup focuses mostly on general parenting issues; The Family Education Network has a wealth of resources for building academic growth in home environments. The writing at both of these sites is lively, and the advice is practical and down-to-earth.

> Family Education Network: www.familyeducation.com
> Parent Soup: www.parentsoup.com

Professional Curriculum Organizations

These Web sites are run by national organizations of teachers with specialized interests in different subject areas (math, science, reading/language arts). They have practical tips suitable for use in newsletters, as well as activities for fostering curricular understanding in parents.

> National Council of Teachers of English (NCTE): www.ncte.org
> National Council of Teachers of Mathematics (NCTM): www.nctm.org
> National Science Teachers Association (NSTA): www.nsta.org

Government Sites

The United States government, through the ERIC database, runs the National Parent Information Network, a rich resource for innovative programs, grant resources, and other parent resource materials. The National Center for Family Literacy also includes an amazing array of materials to support parent involvement in schools.

> National Parent Information Network: www.ericps.ed.uiuc.edu.npin
> National Center for Family Literacy: www.famlit.org

Miscellaneous Sites

Most of the major teaching and parenting magazines run Web sites with sample articles and advice. One of the oldest and most comprehensive is the Web site of Scholastic, the publisher of *Instructor* and *Early Childhood Today* magazines, at: www.scholastic.com

For terrific media materials and updates on the best children's programming, as well as general advice on coping with children's media, visit: www.kidsnet.org

For an example of a fine community-based Web site designed to assist parents and teachers in working with children, visit the Cincinnati, Ohio, "All About Kids" Web site, a treasure trove of tips, research tidbits, articles, and resources worthy of a national audience: www2.aak.com

---

Figure 6   *Best Web Sites for Parent Outreach Materials*

Chapter 4

ADVICE FROM TEACHERS FOR COMMUNICATING WITH PARENTS

As you think about how to increase parents' involvement in your classroom and school, you'll need to consider the big picture of how these essays and newsletters fit into the larger realm of all parent outreach you've planned for the year. Many teachers have some sort of regular two-way written communication with parents built into their parent outreach plan. The key is to come up with a plan that is manageable and respects that some parents will be more involved than others.

Most teachers who have a successful year-long dialogue with parents start from the same set of principles. If you do similar preliminary thinking about your outreach design, you'll be more likely to launch a program that you can sustain throughout the year.

1. *Spend time first thinking about what your goals are for parent outreach.* Consider what "work" you want your home-school communication to do, and don't expect that it can meet all the goals you have for parent outreach. It may be enough to establish communication that informs parents of academic goals, at least at the start. It may be most important for you to get to know the family's attitude toward teachers and schooling a little more. Whatever your goals, keep them focused and simple. This will help you make good choices about how to use your time and how to build your parent outreach program in future months.

2. *Set aside some time for communication with parents.* Decide how much time you can spend on responding to parents, and then stick to it. Don't feel guilty if you only have an hour a week to respond to home-school logs or to put together informational materials for parents. An hour a week will lead to lots of new communication, and it will open doors with parents. For example, an hour is enough time to jot a sentence response to each parent at least once every two weeks, or to send home a weekly essay from this guide with a personal note for just a few parents each week. Parents will be thrilled to get a personal response from a teacher regularly.

3. *Don't limit your expectations for response from parents.* Expand your concept of "parent" outreach to include "family" outreach. In some families, it is more likely that a grandparent or even an older child will respond in a home-school journal. It all depends upon the dynamics of the family. In families where English is not the language used at home, older children will often assist in writing or responding to missives from school. A message from home, no matter who is the author, provides a window into understanding what life is like in the child's home—who does most of the reading and writing, and who is the most important caregiver for your student at different points in the day and evening.

Here are some additional practical tips from teachers at many different grade levels who have developed ongoing, consistent strategies for communicating with parents. You'll notice many do have a dialogue with parents; others choose to meet their communication goals through newsletters. You can use their plans as a starting point for designing your own outreach agenda for the year:

> I send home a behavior and an academic comment report for the week with spelling homework. There are spaces for teacher comments and parent comments. The parents need to sign and return the report. The children are pleased to get homework every week and are proud of the report and their achievements.
> **Marilyn Chesley, Second-Grade Teacher**

> I send home manila folders every Friday. The folders contain school work, notices, and menus. Stapled to the inside cover is a parent-teacher comment sheet—one row for each week of the ranking period. It's a concise means for commenting and keeping parents informed. Folders are returned on Monday.
> **Pam Taylor, Third-Grade Teacher**

> At the beginning of the year, I mail a parent questionnaire and letter to introduce myself to parents of second graders. It includes three questions: (1) Tell me about your child. (2) What would you like me to know about your child in school? (3) What are your expectations for your child? I get lots of information about each child

before the first day. After about two weeks, I write a narrative responding to each parent about the questions and my observations.
> **Barbara Libby, Second-Grade Teacher**

> I send home a weekly newsletter, and I have a parent contact journal where I note *any* conversations (phone, note, in person).
> **Sue Pidhurney, Kindergarten and Reading Recovery Teacher**

> I have math, science, and reading nights with parents, with activities set up that mirror what we'll be doing in the classroom.
> **Mary Ann Colby, Kindergarten Teacher**

> My weekly newsletter includes highlights of the week, children's illustrations, things to remember for next week, and children's personal contributions. Parents are positive, and I have the children do as much of it as possible.
> **Ann Hurd, Second-Grade Teacher**

> I like to do weekly newsletters with children's writing samples. The newsletter is not about what we did today, but rather specific skills and themes that were generated through observations and children's needs.
> **Tracy Forbes, Kindergarten Teacher**

Chapter 5

MAKING INVOLVEMENT EASIER FOR PARENTS

Increasing parent involvement in schools is seldom a simple task, and many of the gains in parent understanding from using these essays, developing newsletters, and fostering more written and oral communication with parents will be hard to measure. They are like the streams running underground that we tap into with wells—we all depend upon them, but they can't be seen.

But while we know written communication does good work in reaching parents, we all want to see more parents attend school events, too. Increases in attendance at school events can be measured, and it builds everyone's confidence that the parent outreach program is succeeding. Answers to the following questions can help you and your school determine if you are doing all you can to help more parents attend school events.

Do we provide free child care?

Many parents have more than one child, or raise their children alone. It can be difficult, if not impossible, for them to attend informational meetings if there is no one to tend to their children at home. Consider enlisting help to provide on-site care for parent information meetings. Possibilities include enlisting the help of the local high school honor society, or designating some funds from the Parent-Teacher Organization to hire competent adults to provide coverage for an hour or two. If you have a discreet "Donations Gratefully Accepted to Support Cost of Child Care Program" box

near the door, you'll probably find the costs of the program are more than covered by participants who can afford to help.

Do we have a master calendar of events in our school?

Many teachers schedule special events and informational meetings in isolation from each other. If more of these events can be scheduled at the same time, on the same night (with child care provided), it makes it possible for parents with more than one child to attend more events.

Do we announce events repeatedly, through multiple forums?

With a master calendar and many vehicles of communication (school and classroom newsletters, phone calls, and notes in home-school journals), parents who are reluctant to attend school events will be reminded how welcome they are at school events, and how very much the school community wants their involvement.

Do we have a way to keep track of parent volunteers?

Because many teachers solicit parent volunteers on their own, sometimes parents who volunteer to provide specialized assistance find their offers are not needed immediately, or are even inadvertently lost in the shuffle. Consider sending out a schoolwide survey once or twice a year so parents can list their talents and when/how they are willing to volunteer in the school (see Figures 7A and 7B). Someone on the school staff (perhaps even a parent volunteer) can compile a master list of parent talents and abilities using keywords and codes. That way, when a third-grade teacher is looking in March for a guest speaker during her "Bugs" unit, she can call up the database and discover there is an entomologist mom of a first grader who would be happy to come in and share her expertise.

It takes a special effort to compile the database, but it is worth it. Teachers understandably can't possibly keep track of all the parent assistance available, especially if some parent talents are unique or available only periodically. Having a schoolwide database can help make the most of parent expertise and enthusiasm.

Do we balance positive and negative comments for all parents?

If some parents only receive phone calls or notes about their child that are negative, they are only likely to appear at parent conferences or other school events under duress. Whenever teachers write a negative note to a parent or make a phone call to report troublesome behavior, they should keep track of the communication. These negative reports should be balanced with some positive communication so parents know that their child's strengths, as well as weaknesses, are being observed. Positive phone

calls and notes also make parents more receptive to the bad news that sometimes needs to be conveyed.

Do we provide a translator for non-English speakers?

Making sure informational materials are sent to parents in their native language, as well as emphasizing what support you have on-site, will provide many more parents with the incentive to attend events if you have a large population of non-English speakers.

Do we provide physical space for parents and parent resources?

Parents need a sense that they are welcome in schools, and they especially need to know what physical space is available for them. Some lucky schools have the luxury of extra space that allows them to set up a parent resource room. But many schools are already cramped and can't sacrifice a space for parents when even students are being housed in portable classrooms.

Even if spots for learning are at a premium at your school, think about what small area you can allocate for parent books and breaks. It may be a "Parent Resource Nook" in the school library, or a bookshelf in the teacher workroom that's festooned with signs that trumpet your appreciation for parent involvement. Many parents spend most of the time in their child's classroom anyway, but it does wonders for morale to see space allocated for parent needs.

Welcome to another wonderful year at Evergreen Elementary School! Our school is part of the community, and we appreciate all the assistance community members give us as volunteers. We also realize that many parents work and may be unable to volunteer during the school day. Please fill out the form below to help us tap into the rich array of expertise that families of our students bring to the school.

And even if you can't volunteer to assist at the school in the day or evening, we know many of you are hard-working volunteers at home, assisting your children with reading and math facts. That's the most important work of all in helping children in our school thrive academically and socially.

If you can't volunteer this year, consider inviting a grandparent, aunt, uncle, friend, or other relation to assist us. Many of our most faithful volunteers are retired people who enjoy being with children.

Thanks for your response!

Volunteer Name _____

School _____

Phone _____

Child's Name _____

When are you able to volunteer? Circle choice or choices

MORNING   AFTERNOON   EVENING

What day or days are best for you to volunteer?

Morning and Afternoon Volunteers
Check the classroom volunteer activities you would be willing to assist with:

_____ assist teacher

_____ guest speaker. Topic(s): _____

_____ clerical

_____ tutor/mentor

_____ home assistant

_____ library assistant

_____ chaperone field trips/social events

_____ translation materials. Language proficiencies: _____

_____ career exploration

_____ lunch buddy program

_____ volunteer office/parent resource center staffing

Evening Volunteers
Check the volunteer activities you would be willing to assist with:

_____ phone tree

_____ evening event goodies

_____ clerical

_____ desktop publishing of class/student books

_____ book orders

_____ parent mentor program

Figure 7A   *Parent Survey I*

Evergreen School has happy news! We have just received funding to create a Parent Resource Room. This resource room will have a computer available for use by parent volunteers who assist in our desktop publishing program. It will also be a comfortable space with a library stocked with books for parents to read on-site or check out. We want this resource center to meet your needs. By taking a few moments to fill out the survey below, you can help us spend our money wisely—as well as assist us in figuring out how to expand the possibilities for our parent outreach program in the future.

What kinds of books should be available in the resource center? You can list topics that interest you, or suggest specific titles.

What hours should the resource center be open?

What other materials (audiotapes, videotapes, software) would you suggest that we purchase?

Would you be willing to volunteer for work in the resource center?

We are expanding our program of workshops for parents. Please check the topics that interest you:

_____ children's self-esteem

_____ dealing with sibling rivalry

_____ healthy eating cooking demonstration

_____ alternatives to television for families

_____ reading to children

_____ helping your child in math

other(s)—list topics: _____

Would you like to be on a phone tree so that other parents can contact you about school events?

Yes   No

Thank you for your response!

[Both parent surveys were adapted from forms used in School Administrative District #1 Presque Isle Region, Maine]

Figure 7B   *Parent Survey II*

Chapter 6

CREATIVE EVENTS FOR PARENTS

If your program for parents has been centered on open houses, science fairs, and parent-teacher conferences, you might want to consider adding a few events to the outreach plan to draw in more parents. Some of these events are designed for whole-school involvement—others work well in individual classrooms.

In thinking about whole-school events, it helps to coordinate the outreach across grade levels early in the year. For example, one classroom or grade might be responsible for one event each year. If the second-grade class is designated to be the "hosts" for Family Science Night, the school has a built-in group of children, teachers, and parent volunteers who have a higher level of interest for the event.

Responsibilities for the host group could include creating all publicity materials, working with the Parent-Teacher Organization to gather and serve refreshments, and soliciting local businesses for door prizes and other support. Designating one group of students and teachers for each event as a "sponsor" fosters a healthy pride in school events and individual recognition of efforts, and it allows the workload to be shared. In addition, you'll find renewed enthusiasm for different events throughout the school year as students, teachers, and parent volunteers find creative ways to reach out for support.

Don't underestimate the value of refreshments, door prizes, and raffles for promoting attendance at creative events, either. If you have free chances for winning prizes, filled out when family members enter the front door, you will boost attendance. Link the prizes to the theme of the event—art supplies for an art fair, books for a "Family Reading Night," math games for a math event.

There is a fine line between building parent event traditions at your school, and getting into a comfortable rut. As you try new events, think about what other events you've done for years. Some of these might be due for some updating, or you might even take a break for a year or two to see if anyone in the school community misses them. Even terrific events can become overused and stale if held year after year. The following section lists some creative events for parents that are growing in popularity.

Family Nights

These events are often focused on a theme—for example, "Family Math Night," "Family Writing Night," or "Family Science Night." Art and reading are popular themes for these nights, too. Teachers set up various centers of activities for parents and children to move between. Depending upon the purposes of the evening, there may be time limits at each station and some whole-group discussion time, or a very informal atmosphere that allows participants to move freely throughout the room.

Because some parents are uncomfortable with their academic abilities in subject areas such as math or science, teachers might want to start with a simple "Family Night" that includes common games that families are familiar with, as well as enjoyable craft activities. Stations can be set up with checkers, Monopoly, Scrabble, building blocks, and art supplies—along with simple placards at each station that highlight what learning takes place through the activity (e.g., spatial intelligence development through the building blocks station; economic awareness through Monopoly).

"First Day" Celebrations

"First Day" events are growing in popularity across the country. Tied to the first day of school in local communities, they can be simple affairs or elaborate collaborations between local businesses, schools, and service organizations. If you are launching a new parent outreach program, First Day celebrations are a wonderful way to bring in many parents and other community members to the school to fill out informational brochures and become familiar with the school and its goals. For more information and a free packet of materials for designing a "First Day" event, e-mail national organizers at firstday@sover.net, visit the First Day Web site at www.firstday.org, or write to First Day Foundation, 210 Main Street, PO Box 10, Bennington, VT 05201.

Community Festivals

To increase participation in big schoolwide celebrations, bring your school into arenas that families enjoy together. Local malls are often willing to host some sort of art festival. Large chain bookstores (like Borders or WaldenBooks) will host school events tied to reading and writing. Consider a simple music concert or talent show in a local park before the first frost. You can also have a sign-up table for parent volunteers at these events. Attendance at these events is often outstanding, since families are able to combine two activities. They can view the art and/or listen to young writers while shopping, or they can listen to the music while enjoying a picnic and socializing.

Readers' Teas

Fall and spring are great times for readers' teas—a chance for students to share what they have been reading with their families in a gracious, genteel discussion group. Teas are particularly popular with grandparents—you might try a "grandparents-only" program, enlisting "foster grandparents" from local seniors groups to befriend children who don't have grandparents in the local area.

Getting Tight with Technology

Invite families in for an afternoon or evening of learning how to operate a computer, accessing the Internet, or setting up e-mail accounts. Include low- and no-cost Internet options, like free service providers (who cover their costs with advertising), or information on when computer clusters are available at the local library. As much as possible, have students lead the workshops and show parents hands-on work at the computer.

Fair Oaks School (in Redwood City, California) even has a computer lending program—families are welcome to take home computers for a week at a time. That's ambitious, but it's worth considering when writing grant proposals specifically geared toward expanding home-school technology links.

Cultural Cookout

Have families bring a dish that represents their culture, as well as the recipe. Recipes can then be collected in a school recipe book, which can be sold to raise funds for additional parent outreach programs.

Community Cleanup

Bring families together to clean up the school grounds and school neighborhood, to plant flowers in the spring, to add fresh paint to classrooms, or to start a recycling program. The cleanup can be combined with an informational program—link the flower planting with a presentation by a commercial gardener; have someone from the recycle center explain where and how recycled materials are used.

Family Band and Orchestra Night

Invite families in for an informal evening of playing instruments, singing, and performing in any way. You can ensure a smooth start to the event by lining up a few talented parents to begin who are comfortable with performing, or have a piano-playing or guitar-strumming parent lead a sing-along.

Nutrition Night

Schedule a presentation or workshop with a local nutritionist—talk about cutting fat from the diet and healthy fast food alternatives (e.g., KFC roasted chicken without the skin as opposed to the traditional recipe with the skin).

Include intriguing facts—a bag of french fries every week for a year has the fat equivalent of sixty-five sticks of margarine. Parents might be treated to healthy quick and easy dinners or snacks that they can prepare with their kids—or that their kids can make on their own. Simple snack preparation can close out the evening.

School Rummage Sale

One community member's trash is another one's treasure. Families can clean out their closets and get a tax deduction for donations. Schools keep all the proceeds and put them into parent outreach programs.

Author's Fairs

Kids read aloud and display their own publications. Schools can also invite local authors in to meet kids and sign books. This is a good event to tie to a family book exchange, with parents and kids contributing books already read (or outgrown as a child ages) that can be traded for titles from other families.

Chapter 7

STRATEGIES FOR INVOLVING NON-ENGLISH-SPEAKING PARENTS

Many teachers face the additional challenge of working with parents who speak English as a second language and are learning their way around both oral and written English. In working with parents who are English-learners, there are a number of strategies that are especially helpful in building bridges between home and school.

Visit the home.

While home visits are time-consuming, in homes where English is the second language a visit can provide more information than any other experience. When you visit the home, you can observe the student interacting with parents and other family members to gain a sense of how ideas from school are translated to home, and what that will mean for future communication.

To make these visits less stressful for all involved, keep them very short and informal. Terri Austin, a teacher in Fairbanks, Alaska, spends either a full day on one Saturday or two evenings early in the fall doing visits to all the homes of her students. She is able to accomplish more than twenty visits in seven hours because she never stays more than thirty minutes at a home and often pops in for five minutes or less. She informs families in a note early in the year that she will be "dropping by" to visit families from 9:00 A.M. to 4:00 P.M. on a particular Saturday. Even such short visits provide amazing insights into family life.

Translate key information from newsletters into the native language.

Solicit volunteers who are proficient in the native language to assist in translations. These volunteers might also visit the homes of parents to see if the materials you are sending home are being used and understood—sometimes the barriers are more cultural than linguistic, and parents who are savvy about these cultural needs can help build your sensitivity to these issues.

Provide translators at school events.

Translators help everyone feel welcome. You can even take the extra step of having a parent proficient in the native language call and encourage parents to come to events—sometimes this intermediary step is what is needed to help English-learners feel at ease.

Purchase additional materials for non-English-speakers in their native language.

Depending upon the language, materials available might be limited. This is not the case for Hispanic parents—there is a wealth of resources for both parents and teachers to assist in building home-school rapport. Two of the best nonprofit clearinghouses for materials on connecting Hispanic parents to schools are:

ASPIRA Association, Inc.
Parent Leadership Programs
1444 Eye Street NW, Suite 800
Washington, DC 20005
Phone: 202-835-3600
Fax: 202-835-3613
E-mail: aspira1@aol.com
URL: www.incacorp.com/aspira/

Hispanic Policy Development Project
1001 Connecticut Ave, NW
Washington, DC 20036
Phone: 202-822-8414
Fax: 202-822-9120
E-mail: jlgar@erols.com

One of the best resources for information on working with immigrant children is:

Clearinghouse for Immigrant Education (CHIME)
c/o National Coalition of Advocates for Students
100 Boylston Street, Suite 737
Boston, MA 02116
Phone: 1-800-441-7192
Web site: www.ncas1.org

CHIME has a limited amount of materials available in Haitian Creole and Vietnamese, as well as numerous Spanish-translated materials. But their best service is providing up-to-date and well-written flyers and short texts on the rights of immigrant children, and the responsibilities of teachers and schools in working with children from diverse backgrounds. Understanding these responsibilities is often the first step in making adaptations to a parent outreach program.

Chapter 8

RESOURCES FOR INVOLVING PARENTS IN SCHOOLS

Books

There are many books that have been published to help teachers involve parents more in schools. The books suggested in Figure 8 will help you think about ways to expand parent involvement. Each one has a different focus. You may want to set different goals, year by year, for increasing parent involvement. For example, a special focus the first year might be involving more families from homes where English is not the native tongue. A big goal another year might be involving more men in your parent outreach plan, or focusing on health and wellness issues in your family events throughout the year. These books are also useful for teacher inservice discussion groups geared toward increasing parent involvement in schools.

AFTER-SCHOOL AND PARENT EDUCATION PROGRAMS FOR AT-RISK YOUTH AND THEIR FAMILIES: A GUIDE TO ORGANIZING AND OPERATING A COMMUNITY-BASED CENTER FOR BASIC EDUCATIONAL SKILLS, REINFORCEMENT, HOMEWORK ASSISTANCE, CULTURAL ENRICHMENT, AND A PARENT INVOLVEMENT FOCUS by Tommie Morton-Young. 1995. Springfield, IL: Charles C. Thomas Books.
Especially useful for understanding the special needs of parents of at-risk youths. Much of the text involves after-school programs, but the activities and suggestions are easily adapted for any type of parent outreach initiative.

THE BIG RED HOW-TO-GUIDE: PLANNING A HEALTH FAIR FOR CHILDREN AND FAMILIES by Christina A. Foley. 1995. Available from National Health and Education Consortium, Institute for Educational Leadership, 1001 Connecticut Avenue, N.W., Suite 310, Washington, DC.
Comprehensive guide for building a wellness and fitness program at a school from scratch.

CHANGING THE VIEW: STUDENT-LED PARENT CONFERENCES by Terri Austin. 1994. Portsmouth, NH: Heinemann.
This brief and well-written text outlines a program that sixth-grade teacher Terri Austin developed for involving students and parents fully in the evaluation process. Chock-full of practical strategies and information.

CREATING SUPPORT FOR EFFECTIVE LITERACY INSTRUCTION by Connie Weaver, Lorraine Gillmeister-Krause, and Grace Vento-Zogby. 1996. Portsmouth, NH: Heinemann.
Excellent workshop resources for educating parents about innovative literacy instruction and helping parents understand literacy development in general.

GETTING MEN INVOLVED: STRATEGIES FOR EARLY CHILDHOOD PROGRAMS by James A. Levine. 1993. New York: Families and Work Institute.
Practical suggestions for increasing the involvement of fathers in parent outreach programs. Though the book covers programs from birth to age eight, there are special sections outlining programs for school-age children and their fathers.

Figure 8   *Annotated Booklist for Parents*

THE HOME-SCHOOL CONNECTION by Jacqueline McGilp and Maureen Michael. 1994. Portsmouth, NH: Heinemann.
Simple and straightforward explanation of the key components of parent involvement programs. The authors are from Australia, but the principles are useful worldwide.

KEEPSAKES: USING FAMILY STORIES IN ELEMENTARY CLASSROOMS by Linda Winston. 1997. Portsmouth, NH: Heinemann.
A practical and thoughtful guide for integrating family stories and the heritage of students throughout the daily life of the classroom and curriculum.

MORE THAN BAKE SALES by James Vopat. 1998. York, ME: Stenhouse.
THE PARENT PROJECT by James Vopat. 1996. York, ME: Stenhouse.
Both of these books by Jim Vopat chronicle The Parent Project, an ongoing program of workshops for parents in literacy developed in Milwaukee, Wisconsin. Especially useful for detailed outlines of workshops that can lead parents to new awareness of key curricular concepts through their own learning.

PARENTS AND SCHOOLS: A SOURCE BOOK. Garland Reference Library of Social Science; Vol. 775 and SOURCE BOOKS ON EDUCATION; Vol. 37 by Angela L. Carrasquillo and Clement B. G. London. 1993. Hamden, CT: Garland Publishing.
A wealth of information about existing innovative programs for parent involvement— especially strong in detailing how to provide support for minority populations.

PARENTS AS PARTNERS IN EDUCATION: FAMILIES AND SCHOOLS WORKING TOGETHER by Eugenia Hepworth Berger. 1994. Columbus, OH: Prentice Hall.
A comprehensive sourcebook of principles and examples of exemplary programs for working with parents.

SCHOOL AND FAMILY PARTNERSHIPS: CASE STUDIES FOR REGULAR AND SPECIAL EDUCATORS by Judith Brachman Buzzell. 1996. Albany, NY: Delmar Publishers.
Shows a variety of ways to build home-school partnerships—particularly relevant for working with parents of special needs children.

WHAT THE OUTGOING PARENT ASSOCIATION PRESIDENT SHOULD HAVE TOLD THE INCOMING PARENT ASSOCIATION PRESIDENT by Lillian Lopez et al.
An essential guide for parent leaders, with information on everything from finances to organizing meetings. This book is hard to find—currently it is only available through the Network of Educators on the Americas catalogue. You can call 1-202-238-2379 for ordering information, or write to: NECA Box 73038 Washington, DC 20056.

Figure 8   *Annotated Booklist for Parents, continued*

Nonprofit Clearinghouses and Service Organizations

A number of nonprofit research and service organizations publish a wide array of parent outreach materials, advice, and support. The following organizations can provide schools with a full list of low-cost publications, including books, newsletters, research reports, videotapes, and parent training materials for schools:

National Center for Family Literacy
325 West Main Street, Suite 200
Louisville, KY 40202-4251
Phone: 502-584-1133
Web site: www.famlit.org

National Parent Teacher Association (PTA)
330 North Wabash Avenue, Suite 2100
Chicago, IL 60611
Phone: 312-670-6782
Fax: 312-670-6783
Web site: www.pta.org

Chapter 9

BEST BOOKS FOR PROMOTING LEARNING AT HOME

If you can afford to create a library of resource materials for parents, there are plenty of good titles available to stock (see Figure 9). In putting it together, you'll want to:

• *Balance academic materials with affective titles.* Until recently, books for parents were heavily weighted toward affective (or general parenting) issues. In the past few years, many more books have been published to help parents foster academic achievement in children, too. Many of the academic or learning-oriented titles listed in Figure 9 have suggested activities that are suitable for Family Night events at schools or for inclusion in take-home project bags that students can complete with families.

• *Emphasize books with short, practical information.* Parents often prefer books that are packed with activities, quick tips, and helpful hints that are easy to understand. These books are also loaded with short items that you can use in newsletters, too.

Realize that you will lose some books in your library if you loan them out regularly—it's inevitable. You can spend lots of time policing the library and returns, or you can accept that a portion of your library will be lost annually. When parents ask what gifts are needed in the classroom, you can tactfully give them suggestions for books to replenish your parent library.

Academic Titles

A+ PARENTS: HELP YOUR CHILD LEARN AND SUCCEED IN SCHOOL by Adrienne Mack. September 1997. Ithaca, NY: McBooks Press.

CHILD'S PLAY 6–12: 160 INSTANT ACTIVITIES, CRAFTS AND SCIENCE PROJECTS FOR GRADE SCHOOLERS by Leslie Hamilton. 1997. New York: Three Rivers Press.

THE CONNECTED FAMILY: BRIDGING THE DIGITAL GENERATION GAP by Seymour Papert. 1996. Marietta, GA: Longstreet.

DOING ART TOGETHER: DISCOVERING THE JOYS OF APPRECIATING AND CREATING ART AS TAUGHT AT THE METROPOLITAN MUSEUM OF ART'S FAMOUS PARENT-CHILD WORKSHOP by Muriel Silberstein-Storfer. 1997. New York: Harry N. Abrams.

50 SIMPLE THINGS YOU CAN DO TO RAISE A CHILD WHO LOVES HISTORY AND GEOGRAPHY (50 SIMPLE THINGS SERIES) by Anne Stribling. 1997. New York: Arco.

50 SIMPLE THINGS YOU CAN DO TO RAISE A CHILD WHO LOVES MATH (50 SIMPLE THINGS SERIES) by Kathy A. Zahler. 1997. New York: Macmillan General Reference.

MATH MAGIC FOR YOUR KIDS by Scott Flansburg. 1997. New York: William Morrow.

Figure 9   *Best Books for Parents*

Academic Titles, continued

ONCE UPON A HEROINE: 450 BOOKS FOR GIRLS TO LOVE by Alison Cooper-Mullin and Jennifer Marmaduke Coye. 1998. Chicago: Contemporary Books.

101 EDUCATIONAL CONVERSATIONS WITH YOUR 2ND GRADER (101 EDUCATIONAL CONVERSATIONS YOU SHOULD HAVE WITH YOUR CHILD) by Vito Perrone. 1992. New York: Chelsea House.

POSITIVE INVOLVEMENT: HOW TO TEACH YOUR CHILD HABITS FOR SCHOOL SUCCESS by Jack Youngblood and Marsha Youngblood. 1995. Greenbelt, MD: Brown Wood.

THE READ-ALOUD HANDBOOK by Jim Trelease. 1996. New York: Simon & Schuster.

365 WAYS TO HELP YOUR CHILD LEARN AND ACHIEVE by Cheri Fuller. 1996. Colorado Springs, CO: Pinon Press.

YOU CAN DO IT! HOW TO BOOST YOUR CHILD'S ACHIEVEMENT IN SCHOOL by Michael Bernard. 1997. New York: Warner Books.

Social/Behavioral Titles

BRAVE NEW GIRLS: CREATIVE IDEAS TO HELP GIRLS BE CONFIDENT, HEALTHY AND HAPPY by Jeannette Gadeberg. 1996. Minneapolis: Fairview Press.

CHORES WITHOUT WARS by Lynn Lott and Riki Intner. 1997. Rocklin, CA: Prima Publishing.

DR. MOM'S PARENTING GUIDE by Marianne Neifert. 1996. New York: Plume Books.

GOOD FRIENDS ARE HARD TO FIND: HELPING YOUR CHILD FIND, MAKE AND KEEP FRIENDS by Fred Frankel. 1996. Pasadena, CA: Perspective Publishing.

HOW TO GIVE YOUR CHILD A GREAT SELF-IMAGE by Deborah Phillips with Fred Bernstein. 1989. New York: Penguin Books.

HOW TO TALK SO KIDS WILL LEARN by Adele Faber, Lisa Nyber, and Rosalyn Anstine Templeton. 1996. New York: Simon & Schuster.

HOW TO TALK SO KIDS WILL LISTEN AND LISTEN SO KIDS WILL TALK by Adele Faber and Elaine Mazlish. 1985. New York: Simon & Schuster.

HOW TO TALK TO YOUR KIDS ABOUT REALLY IMPORTANT THINGS by Charles Schaefer and Theresa Foy DiGeronimo. 1994. San Francisco: Jossey-Bass.

LESSONS FROM DAD: A TRIBUTE TO FATHERHOOD edited by Joan Aho. 1997. Deerfield Beach, FL: Health Communications.

LESSONS FROM MOM: A TRIBUTE TO LOVING WISDOM edited by Joan Aho. 1996. Deerfield Beach, FL: Health Communications.

NAPKINS: LUNCH BAG NOTES FROM DAD by Courtney Garton. 1997. Columbia, MD: Perry Publishing.

PARACHUTES FOR PARENTS: 12 NEW KEYS TO RAISING CHILDREN FOR A BETTER WORLD by Bobbie Sandoz. 1997. Chicago: Contemporary Books.

RAISING LOW-FAT KIDS IN A HIGH-FAT WORLD by Judith Shaw. 1997. San Francisco: Chronicle Books.

THE SEVEN SECRETS OF HIGHLY EFFECTIVE PARENTS by Randy Rolfe. 1998. Chicago: Contemporary Books.

TEMPERAMENT TOOLS: WORKING WITH YOUR CHILD'S INNER TRAITS by Helen Neville and Diane Johnson. 1998. Seattle: Parenting Press.

365 AFTER SCHOOL ACTIVITIES by Sheila Ellison and Judith Barnett. 1998. Napierville, IL: Sourcebooks.

365 TV-FREE ACTIVITIES by Steve and Ruth Bennett. 1996. Holbrook, MA: Adams Media Corporation.

THE WONDER OF BOYS: WHAT PARENTS, MENTORS AND EDUCATORS CAN DO TO SHAPE THEM INTO EXCEPTIONAL MEN by Michael Gurion. 1997. New York: Tarcher/Putnam.

Figure 9   *Best Books for Parents, continued*

Chapter 10

WRITING GRANTS TO SUPPORT PARENT OUTREACH PROGRAMS

The good news is that there *is* money available to support parent outreach programs. The not-so-good news is that the programs often involve one-time-only funding, or are so poorly publicized that schools only hear about them after the money has been awarded. There are ways to increase your chances of gaining funds through any grant competition if you use the following guidelines.

Look at how you're using grants your school has already received.

Certain grant programs like federal funding through Title I require parent involvement and some use of funds to support that involvement. You might consider using some of those funds differently to expand your parent outreach program.

Connect your grant applications.

Title I grants also require that parents and schools write compacts with specific goals. If you can connect future grant applications (particularly for federal funds) to the parent outreach goals already developed in previously funded grants, you are more likely to be seen as having a long-term, sustained plan for outreach. That also means you are more likely to be funded. Take a look at the grants currently awarded to your school and what goal statements are in these grants for parent outreach.

Always try to talk to someone from the funding agency before applying.

The longer and more complicated the grant application is (and the higher the potential funding), the more crucial this chat will be. Many proposal guidelines are very vague. Talking with a grant officer will help you determine if there are unwritten preferences in the funding agency. For example, a grant officer might let you know that many grants in the previous year were funded to help schools build parent resource libraries. The agency might have a preference this year for funding workshop programs. Similarly, the grant program may give preference to schools that provide some matching funds or are in underserved areas—all information that may or may not be on the application form. Key questions to ask a grant officer include:

1. What percentage of applications are funded?
2. What was the distribution of grants the previous year?
3. Are names and phone numbers of any previous grant recipients available?
4. Is there a process for getting support in reapplication if a grant is turned down?

Many agencies give special consideration to schools or individuals who make the effort to rewrite their applications the following year after getting advice from the agency—the funding rate for applicants who show this kind of persistence in asking for additional guidance can be very high.

Keep your application simple and eye-pleasing.

No fancy fonts or formatting or odd-colored paper should be used for your grant proposal—save your creativity for your school newsletter! Also, use a large, easy to read font. Don't give in to the temptation to cram as much information as possible on the page. Many grant applicant reviewers are members of the bifocal club—larger fonts and simple designs unconsciously promote some applications over other requests that are just as worthy but hard to read.

Think about your needs before you begin applying for grants.

As you meet with Parent-Teacher Organizations early in the year, or work with colleagues to design a new parent outreach program, think about the ways that funding could help you meet your goals. Most grant applications require a narrative explanation of why the funds will be needed and how they will be used. You can write a "master narrative" early in the year that details what funding is needed and how it will be used. This narrative can then be revised for use in different programs, tailored to the constraints of the grant program. See Figure 10 for a sample master narrative, as well as Figure 11 for examples of insert paragraphs that were used for different grant applications.

Compile a creative "wish list" of needs.

Many grant competitions limit the kinds of materials and resources they will fund, so you'll want to have a master "wish list" of all the ways you could use financial support in your outreach program. That way you can quickly scan the list, tailoring your budget request to the constraints of each grant competition. Potential budget requests might include:

1. Professional books/videotapes/CDs for training teachers
2. Instructional books/videotapes/CDs for training parents
3. Funding for a resource library for parents
4. Children's books/resources for a loaner library for parents
5. Release time (paid substitutes) to allow teachers to do parent training during the school day
6. Refreshments for events
7. Paid child care at events
8. Paid translators to convert school materials into other languages for non-English speakers
9. Photocopy/advertising costs
10. Computer for parent workroom/newsletter formatting/parent database
11. Funds for senior/family lunch special events
12. Paid attendance for parents at professional conferences (as part of school team)
13. Funds for Parent/Teacher/Administration Planning Retreat
14. Funding for Home-School Outreach Coordinator (part- or full-time)
15. Craft supplies/materials for Family Night events

For more information on funding parent outreach programs, you might want to consult *Funding a Family Literacy Program*, a guide available at a cost of $12 from the National Center for Family Literacy. Write to:

National Center for Family Literacy
Attn: Publications
325 W. Main Street, Suite 200
Louisville, KY 40202
Phone: (502) 584-1133
Fax: (502) 584-0172

Use strong verbs in your narrative.

Nothing pumps up the quality of writing more than strong verbs. Look to replace as many nonactive verbs in your narrative as possible with creative, energized words.

Much recent research shows the importance of involving parents in school programs. Studies have demonstrated that there is a direct correlation between parent involvement and student achievement. Federal initiatives such as the federal Goals 2000 program emphasize the need for more involvement by parents in schools, beginning with programs that can assist parents in understanding how to link school learning with learning at home.

Elm Street Elementary School has enacted an ambitious three-year plan for increasing parent involvement in our school. This plan includes:

- developing a parent resource library and workroom
- initiating a new weekly newsletter that goes out to all parents
- launching monthly "Family Nights" to bring more parents into the school to learn about the curriculum
- sponsoring a schoolwide arts festival to be held in the spring at a local mall
- compiling a database of parent interests, needs, and volunteer efforts
- providing child care support and Spanish translators at all schoolwide functions
- providing free passes to senior citizens for lunches during the school day with students

This plan was designed by a committee of parent volunteers, administrators, and teachers working together. Parents were surveyed first to get information about their needs, and then the survey results were used in a series of meetings throughout the spring to create a new parent outreach program.

Success of the program will be measured in a variety of ways, including conducting annual surveys of parents (to provide quantitative and qualitative measures of program success); tracking attendance at school events; conducting focus group interviews in the spring of the second year with randomly selected parents; and gathering annual written evaluations by teachers of the effects of the program on parent involvement.

[INSERT PARAGRAPH(S) HERE, TAILORED TO SPECIFIC GRANT COMPETITION. See Figure 11.]

We believe this is the most important outreach program we have ever initiated at our school. Thank you for considering our request for funding.

Figure 10   *Grant Application Master Narrative*

Repeat specific phrases from the call for applications in your proposal.

It's important for the grant committee to see that your proposal is directly linked to the goals and aims of its program. Make that task easy for them by using specific references from their own literature. Highlight in some way the words or phrases from the specific grant program you are applying to in your narrative. The sample insert paragraphs (Figure 11) have the key phrases from the grant call for proposals highlighted in italicized type—this will draw the review committee's attention to the connections between the application and the funding priorities of the program.

A little advance preparation can lead to much more funding for your school. Remember that if your school received a call for grant proposals only three days before the proposals were due, most other schools are working with just as little time as you. Grant programs that are the least well-organized and well-publicized often have the highest percentage of proposals funded.

For a grant competition from the Statewide Chamber of Commerce:

We are requesting funds to support the schoolwide arts festival, to be held this spring at a local mall. Your call for proposals states that funds will be awarded *"to programs that best connect local educational programs with business partnerships."* Many local Chamber of Commerce members are already providing gifts and small amounts of money to support this event. By moving the arts festival from school to the local mall, we will bring student work and families who view this work into the local community. Funds would also be used to bring in people from local businesses with an arts connection (e.g., a symphony member guest will speak with a third-grade class about music, a graphic designer from the local newspaper will talk to first graders about integrating words and pictures) in the week before the arts festival.

For a grant competition involving a state program to support programs for parents of students with special needs:

We are requesting funds to support the development of our parent resource library and workroom. Your call for proposals requires that all grant applications *"demonstrate how the program will build communication between parents of children with special needs and the larger school community."* We are requesting funds for books and videotapes for parents of special needs children. A list of titles to be purchased is included on the budget sheet. Funding would also be used to sponsor two workshops in the workroom for special needs parents. These workshops would have two purposes. First, they would introduce parents to the books and videotapes available. Second, they would allow parents to meet others who share some of their concerns and experiences, building a network of support.

From an application for resources to support needs of non-English speakers:

We are requesting funds to support the development of a resource base of materials translated into Spanish and Vietnamese. Your call for proposals requires that grant applications *"demonstrate how the program will reach underserved populations in the school community."* By finding translation services for weekly newsletters, as well as the development of a mentoring program for Hispanic- and Vietnamese-speaking parents, we will enhance communication with these groups.

Figure 11   *Sample Grant Insert Paragraphs*

Chapter 11

WRITING FOR PARENTS AND THE LARGER COMMUNITY

Once you've honed your writing skills a bit by creating newsletters and flyers for parents, you might want to consider trying to reach more community members through local media.

In deciding when to approach the media, understanding a bit about how people get their news might be helpful. A recent Pew Research Center survey of three thousand adults demonstrates the value of reaching out to different media sources with information about your outreach programs:

- One-third of eighteen- to twenty-nine-year-olds said they enjoy keeping up with the news.
- Only 28 percent had read a newspaper the day before the pollster's call, but print media continues to be the most important source of news for the best-educated and most affluent audiences.
- The local, not national, 11:00 P.M. television news was the biggest source of television news information for adults.
- Morning radio programs reach more people (e.g., commuters) than television or newspapers.

These statistics show that there are many ways to reach parents through the media, and that there is no one single "best way" to ensure that your message reaches a larger audience.

Classroom Newsletters and Flyers

The easiest way to spark interest in your events is regularly to mail out copies of your classroom newsletters or flyers announcing events to local newspapers, television stations, and radio stations, highlighting what you think will be newsworthy. Make a master list of local newspaper, radio station, and television station addresses. Always address any correspondence to the "Education Reporter." Local media have such a large regular turnover in staff that it usually isn't worth the bother to try to figure out the name of the current education reporter.

News Releases

If you have the time, or if there is a special event you really hope will receive coverage, you might send a news release to local media (see Figure 12). News releases are often used to announce events on morning radio programs, and smaller newspapers will print them almost word for word if space allows. Larger newspapers will use them as a start for gathering information for their own stories.

News releases can also snag the interest of television news programs. Many family members still gather around the television for the local news each evening. Your ability to get a local news crew interested in an event at your school in large part is determined by the size of the community you live in. Competition is fierce in large cities for news time—it's much easier to get coverage in smaller communities. But you might be surprised at what local stations find newsworthy.

The release should be limited to one page in length, and it should include:

NEWS RELEASE

Evergreen Woods, IA: Can math instruction include games of Monopoly and surveying how many children like bologna sandwiches? It can if the program is "Family Math Night" at Evergreen Elementary School, to be held on Monday, October 14th from 7:00–8:30 P.M. at the school on Main Street in Evergreen.

The night includes displays of children's work in math throughout the school, sample math problems and brain teasers for families to try in the library, and a variety of math activities for different grade levels in each classroom. Even the school cafeteria staff are helping participants get in a math mood, serving "pound" cake for refreshment.

But it's not all fun and games at "Family Math Night" at Evergreen Elementary School. Children are learning important new math concepts, and parents are learning how to support math learning.

"We know that math is a subject that wasn't lots of fun for many parents when they were in school, but this event changes attitudes," explains Family Math Night coordinator Kim Pennypacker. "Parents enjoy seeing how much their children are learning, and we enjoy building connections between what we do in school and all the important learning going on at home."

The public is welcome to attend, and there is no charge for admission. For further information, contact Kim Pennypacker at 555-1441.

Figure 12   *Sample News Release for Family Math Night at Evergreen School*

- date, location, and title of event in first paragraph (preferably in the first or second sentence)
- second and third paragraphs that explain why the event is important (preferably including a quote or two from an organizer—don't be shy about quoting yourself!)
- a final sentence that includes the name and phone number of a contact person for the event

Don't forget to add the local free "penny saver" newspapers to your mailing lists. Often these newspapers are more widely read than the public realizes, and their small staffs make well-written news releases on local events particularly attractive to them.

Op/Ed Essays

Beyond news releases, you might also consider writing an op/ed essay for your local or state newspaper (see Figure 13). If your op/ed piece is published, you will have parents and citizens with many different perspectives reading your words. These include folks who may vote on your local school budget. Legislators consider-

ing the state and national literacy reform initiatives will also see your viewpoint. If you want your writing to be read (and you can't afford to rent a local billboard!), no outlet has a greater reach than your local newspaper. The following tips can help get your opinions published.

Have a local angle.

The op/ed is much more likely to be published if your points are directly connected to local concerns. Write up a brief draft of your op/ed. Then look daily for letters to the editor or feature stories published about the issue you want to write about. Send your op/ed within a day or so of the publication of the letter or feature. Reference the local story in your lead.

For example, if there is a front-page story extolling the virtues of a new reading program, you can cite that in your op/ed about quality reading instruction locally. A letter to the editor that mentions a fine multiage teacher can be used to support your own op/ed on why multiage instruction is a good option for students and teachers. Op/ed editors are always looking for editorials with a local angle; they already have far more well-written editorials available from nationally syndicated writers than they could ever use.

Last week's *Evergreen Daily News* had a front-page story on the rise in violence in high schools across the country. The same story included information about increases in teen suicides in our region. The state legislature has formed a new task force to consider ways to keep violence out of our schools. Leaders of the task force were quoted as saying violent outbursts in schools were almost inevitable, given the attitude and experiences of youths today.

As an elementary teacher and parent, these news stories trouble me. We all have a role to play in helping teens find their place in the world, and providing help for them as they grow. We need to look for solutions to the problems of youths in the early years of schooling, and support programs that foster healthy social, academic, and emotional growth.

Fortunately, there are many things we can all do to assist the young in our community. Researchers Shirley Brice Heath and Milbrey McLaughlin of Stanford University have studied achievement of youths across many communities in the country, over many years. Their research shows the single greatest factor in determining if youths will grow to be successful, mentally healthy adults is involvement in extracurricular activities throughout their formative years. Sports were found to be a positive influence for many youths. But they found a few other activities were even more significant in promoting positive mental health and academic achievement—these are activities that involve the arts. Youths studied who had regular, group activities around music, art, theater, or dance were most likely to grow up to be caring, committed, and successful citizens.

At a time when youth violence and unhappiness is rising, it's important that we fund programs that we know will counteract these disturbing trends. Children involved in in-school and out-of-school arts programs are doing more than filling their time and being creative—they are developing a strong sense of self and connection to others.

The Evergreen School District, in partnership with local businesses and the Rotary Club, is sponsoring an arts festival next week at the Evergreen Valley Mall. Everyone in the community is invited to stop in sometime during the week of May 12–19 to view the wonderful work of students from our local schools involved in our many arts programs. Displays will also explain the many arts programs volunteers and staff run throughout the year in our schools, including the fall theater revue and summer music camp. The evening of May 12th will feature recognition for our parent volunteers. Each night will also include performances by our school bands, choruses, and theater groups at 7:00 P.M. sharp.

Articles like the ones on the *Evergreen Daily News* front page last week that describe a rise in school violence and teen suicides can make us all feel helpless. But we still have a lot of power to help children find a healthy, productive place in society. Funding for arts programs is a wonderful tool for helping youths find a place in our community. Join us next week at the mall to see just how powerful this tool can be. And when school budgets are voted on next month, make sure you support funding for the arts. Arts funding is not a budget frill—it's essential for any community that wants to help its children grow up healthy, strong, and committed to making the world a better place.

Figure 13   *Community Arts Festival Op/Ed*

E-mail, fax, and use regular mail to submit your work.

It's hard to know which form of communication is used most readily by your local op/ed page editor, so use all three. Many op/ed editors especially like e-mail submissions, because they then have your essay in electronic form. Information for submission is usually right on the editorial page.

Fact check, and provide fact-checking references.

An op/ed piece is more likely to be accepted if you include some facts to back up your points— a few statistical references are particularly appealing to editors in backing up your opinions. But make sure you do your own fact checking. Rather than just referencing a professional journal, it's better to include the name and phone number of the researcher in the article. The same goes for facts from national organizations—include a name and phone number that is accurate. Many media organizations have recently been criticized for poor fact checking. They will appreciate the accuracy of your work if you include names and phone numbers for cross-referencing. A bonus from good fact checking—often editors will use the names listed for interviews for a future feature about the issue you're writing about.

Include the right information in your cover letter.

You need to state on the cover page that your essay has not been published or submitted elsewhere, and sign the cover page. Newspapers can't publish any op/ed without this signed statement. Even if you've e-mailed your submission, you'll need to drop off a signed hard copy of the cover page disclaimer. You should also include a brief (one sentence or less) description of yourself—where you reside and where you work.

Keep it short.

Most op/eds are limited to 500 to 800 words. It's important to stick to the limit. If you go over it by much, your work will not even be considered.

And if a longer op/ed is accepted, you run the risk of the editor making cuts that muddle the points you were trying to make.

For example, the op/ed in Figure 13 does a lot of good work in promoting a school's outreach program for parents. It publicizes a big local event for the community, and it pushes for more arts funding (ideally, right before school budgets will be voted on in this town). And because the publicity is tied to a recent news article in the paper, it is more likely to be accepted by the op/ed editor. This op/ed is 570 words—just right in size for most newspapers.

If you're thinking about reaching out to local media, you might start by brainstorming with your colleagues a list of issues in your school that are most important in the coming year and that are most likely to require some education of the community. Decide which programs would be best publicized by news releases and which are also suitable for an op/ed essay. For example, if you're implementing a new assessment program or science curriculum, a positive op/ed early in the process has the potential to build support and diffuse criticism later. News releases and op/eds in tandem with regular classroom newsletters sent home can do a lot of important work in building support for school innovations.

Chapter 12

FROM PARENT POWER TO COMMUNITY POWER
One School's Story

By now it's possible that your head is spinning with all the possibilities for parent outreach. You might have snatches of phrases in your head to use in a grant proposal, or a good idea for reformatting your newsletter, or the urge to gather some colleagues together for a cup of coffee and a long chat about how to change your parent outreach program. Getting started is often easy, especially if you set reasonable goals individually and as a school. What's always harder is sustaining a parent outreach program. Inspiration comes when you look at what happens when a parent outreach program builds over a period of years, not weeks or months. That is exactly what happened at Mapleton Elementary School in Mapleton, Maine, a school within Maine's School Administrative District #1 (Presque Isle region).

Mapleton is located in the far north of the state. The community is rural and economically depressed, surrounded by potato fields and farmers who have endured years of poor harvests and a steady decrease in demand for their crop. While the local economy may be grim, the community is blessed with a school and teaching staff committed to building ties between school and home.

Seven years ago, teachers on staff began the hard work of building a much stronger parent outreach program. Gail Gibson, a fifth-grade teacher who now serves as the principal of the school, wrote a $1,000 state-funded grant for building community outreach. Instead of spending the money on books or a few special events, the school decided to fund a retreat at a nice resort for eight people—four parents, plus administrators and teachers. Over three days, the group brainstormed all the possibilities for involving families more in schools, as well as solutions to problems that keep parents from becoming involved. Rather than plan just individual events, the group was able to create a comprehensive, multiyear vision and plan—working toward fostering an environment at the school where parents would always feel welcome, involved, and able to talk with school staff about issues as they emerged.

The staff is always looking for funding, and they use small amounts of money as seed money to build larger programs. When Gail noticed there were $75 grants available for parent materials through the federal Goals 2000 initiative, she took a few minutes to work with parents to fill out the application. "It was worth the time, because anyone who sent in the application received the money," she explained. After purchasing some books and reserving some school space for a parent resource workroom, she went to the Parent-Teacher Organization and requested more funding. The whole staff began to look for more funding for materials, using small amounts of funds left over from projects and allocating small amounts of the budgets in other grants for parent materials.

At school events, raffles are held in the parent resource workroom. Local businesses donate gift certificates and prizes. Signs publicize the raffle throughout the school, and teachers urge family members to take a look at the room before leaving. Almost all parents stop by because they want to put their names into the raffle, and the school makes sure there are refreshments offered to keep people in the room a bit longer. Parent volunteers also prowl the hallways, recruiting their friends and neighbors to visit the room and borrow materials. In recent years, many of the new materials in the parent resource library have been donated by the parents themselves. Those who can afford gifts often choose to buy books for the resource room, as a way of helping other parents in the school community.

Beyond newsletters and regular communication with parents, the teachers have worked to develop a mindset of always finding ways to involve more parents in the school. For example, first-grade teacher Joanne Thompson realized there were some parents who were never able to visit during the day. She put together a video with student help of work areas and activities throughout the day in the classroom. That video is sent home to parents, and many comment in writing and through phone calls about how much they enjoy seeing the daily routine.

Teachers save space in the back of student-published books and projects for parent comments, and regularly remind parents to comment. First-grade teacher Lois Pangburn realized that some parents weren't attending events she held during the day, perhaps because they were shy in large groups. In response, she initiated a bimonthly "Readers' Tea," in which only parents of four or five students are invited. Attendance is just about perfect—parents are notified far enough in advance to rearrange work schedules, and children love having their parents there as part of a small, special group. This regular event, held every two weeks, ensures that virtually all parents visit the classroom during the day by the end of the fall.

The teachers are always adapting plans based upon the response from parents. After bemoaning the poor quality of most training materials to help parents understand school issues, the staff decided to use good teacher preparation videos in training parent volunteers. More than forty parents attended a workshop on helping with reading, using a high-quality program developed for teachers. Parents committed to an hour of training for six weeks, with the library open before and after sessions for additional resources to be read at home. Many of these parents have become adept reading tutors, at almost no cost to the school.

The school has also embraced the concept of partnerships with local businesses and service clubs—not just asking for financial support for programs, but looking for ways to work together. When the local Rotary Club was suffering from low membership, the president called the school to let the staff know they might have to cancel their annual Hunter's Breakfast. Gail asked the school staff if they were willing to help in exchange for some of the proceeds. The breakfast was a decades-old tradition, and one of the main events all year for the Club. The whole school staff volunteered to assist, with the Rotary Club happily donating all earnings from the breakfast to parent outreach and other academic support programs at the school. "I can tell you, it sure has an impact on parents when they see teachers flipping pancakes and doling out eggs at 5:00 A.M. on a Saturday," explained Gail. The service club was overjoyed at being able to continue the event, and the school received terrific publicity and a windfall in funding. Following the breakfast collaboration, the grateful service club contributed more than $7,000 to the school's arts in education program over the next few years.

Mapleton's week-long Art Fair at the local mall is mobbed every spring, and the Parent Volunteer Appreciation Night has the best attendance of the week, with free refreshments all evening and periodic announcements of special awards to committed volunteers. All students have at least one piece of art exhibited, and bands, choruses, and theater groups from the high school perform each night.

Parents are not the only family members welcome in the district schools—the whole community knows the doors of the school are open to them. Any senior citizen can receive tickets for a free lunch at the high school, and it's a popular social event for many. More than forty senior citizens go to lunch at the high school each week. It's far less expensive than hiring extra lunch monitors or assigning more lunch duties for teaching staff. Nothing generates better discipline and decorum in students than having your grandma sitting at the lunch table with you. If funding is tight for a program like this in your school, you can always build partnerships with local agencies that provide free lunches to senior citizens.

There are many ways to measure the success of this district's community outreach program. Mapleton last year received the highest possible score on the reading portion of the statewide fourth-grade assessment, ranking it with a handful of school districts throughout the state. Almost all other districts with such high scores were wealthy, spending far more per pupil than Mapleton. For teachers and parents, the high scores on tests are probably the least important measure of the success of the outreach program. Walk through the school on any day of the year, and you'll see parents working one-on-one with children in quiet corners of classrooms. You'll see senior citizens being interviewed by children for an oral history project. An atmosphere of warmth and welcome for community members pervades the school.

It's worth noting that the district has a full-time, paid family-school coordinator and a part-time, paid volunteer coordinator. Much of the development of home-school outreach can be linked to how much the district values community involvement, to the point where they are willing to pay a staff member to coordinate this work. Like fine educators everywhere, teachers throughout the district choose to make the extra effort to write grants and host special events throughout the school year—but they have support from someone who does this work as a full-time job. Other districts might see these types of staff positions as a luxury in times of budget cuts. But for this district, these positions are necessities, their need backed by decades of research nationally that shows how critical family involvement is for student success. Teachers and administrators need only think of the money the school might be spending on high-priced consultants for a new reading program if scores were low. Or they might consider the battles at budget hearings if parents didn't feel welcome in schools, or didn't know how integral the school is for life in the entire community. Even the most frugal Mapleton residents can see that this is money well-spent.

Chapter 13

FINAL THOUGHTS
How Much Does It Cost?

Every parent outreach suggestion in this resource guide has a cost. Some of the suggestions are very low-cost—the price of photocopying an essay to send home to parents or buying a few books to share with families as they try to help their children achieve. Some of the costs are only measured in the time it takes to put together some materials or to put together an event. Even then, it may be difficult for some teachers and schools to justify building outreach programs when so many other essential needs aren't met in schools today.

Maybe we should ponder what price we all pay when parent outreach programs don't connect with most families in our schools. The costs of an unsuccessful parent outreach program can be astronomical—calculated through the number of children and parents who are disenfranchised from schools, in miscommunications and distrust, and in isolation of schools from local citizens when connection is needed more than ever.

Building a comprehensive parent outreach program is expensive—if not in dollars then in time and energy given by school staff. But the expense of *not* having a strong program of communicating and working with parents is far higher. Once schools make a commitment to building their school outreach program, they are often astonished by the results. There is an enormous base of enthusiasm and creativity available if we tap into the lives and interests of the families around us. Parents do want to help in schools, and they do want to know more about how children learn. We all know this—communicating well with parents reminds us of it daily and revitalizes our commitment to children and the larger communities we serve.

Part 2

Parent Essay Masters

Heinemann uses nonsexist language in all materials. In the following reproducible essays, the nonsexist plural is used to refer to individual children (for example, "Your child may put their book bag…" as opposed to "Your child may put his or her book bag…").

Writing at Home

Children have to learn to read before they can learn to write, right? Wrong! Surprisingly, research shows that many kids actually learn to write first—their development as readers comes after they begin to attempt to write letters and words. Practicing letters and sounds freely while drawing and sketching helps build reading ability. That's why many teachers have added longer writing instruction periods to elementary school days over the past decade, and they encourage children to write freely when they draw. If you want to see your child develop as a reader, there is no better activity than writing. Here are things you can do as a parent to help your child enjoy learning to write:

- **Keep paper, pencils, markers, and crayons around.**
  Ask your child what kind of materials they like to write with, and then set up a small storage area that includes some writing supplies.
- **Don't worry about correct spelling too early.**
  Remember that the attempt is what matters with children—if they see you celebrate seeing them put pen to paper, they will want to write more. Children can easily be overwhelmed by too much advice and criticism, no matter how gently it is given.
- **Remember that "writing" is drawing for many young learners.**
  Children will make pictures before they write words. Ask your child to explain what they've drawn to you—the explanation often is a story that is the germ of an idea for writing. And make sure to do a little writing and drawing with your child—you will be amazed at the conversations that take place while you are both sketching and writing together.
- **Treat your child to new writing tools.**
  For a special surprise, buy some nice writing paper on sale, or scented markers you know your child will enjoy. New tools can spark new interest in writing.
- **Let your child help you write.**
  Whenever you're writing down a phone message, grocery list, or note, ask your child if they would like to write with you. Let them write their own version, side by side with you.

   Parent Power by B. Power, © 1999. Portsmouth, NH: Heinemann.

Escribir en la casa

Los niños tienen que aprender a leer antes de aprender a escribir, ¿no es verdad? ¡Falso! Sorpresivamente, las investigaciones muestran que muchos niños realmente aprenden a escribir primero. El desarrollo como lectores viene después de empezar a tratar de escribir letras y palabras. Practicar las letras y sonidos libremente mientras hacen dibujos ayuda a desarrollar la habilidad de lectura en los niños. Es por eso que muchos maestros han añadido períodos de instrucción de escritura más largos al calendario de la escuela primaria durante la pasada década, y por eso alientan a los niños a que escriban libremente cuando dibujan. Si usted quiere ver a su hijo(a) desarrollarse como lector, no hay mejor actividad que escribir. Aquí le señalamos cosas que puede hacer como padre para estimular el gusto por la lectura en su hijo(a):

- **Mantenga a mano papel, lápices, marcadores y creyones.**
  Pregunte a su hijo(a) con qué tipo de materiales le gustaría escribir. Establezca un área pequeña donde guardar los materiales que se necesitan para escribir.
- **No se preocupe por corregir la ortografía demasiado pronto.**
  Recuerde que lo que importa con los niños es el esfuerzo. Si ellos ven que usted los celebra por hacer el esfuerzo, querrán escribir más. A los niños se les puede abrumar fácilmente con muchos consejos y críticas, no importa con qué suavidad se hagan.
- **Recuerde que para muchos que comienzan a aprender, "escribir" es dibujar.**
  Los niños harán dibujos antes de escribir palabras. Pida a su hijo(a) que explique lo que ha dibujado. La explicación quizás sea un cuento que servirá de germen a una idea para escribir. Asegúrese de escribir y dibujar un poco con su hijo(a). Usted se sorprenderá de las conversaciones que tendrán mientras dibujan y escriben.
- **Invite a su hijo(a) a usar materiales nuevos para escribir.**
  Como una sorpresa especial, compre algún papel de escribir bonito que esté en venta, o marcadores perfumados que usted sabe que le gustan a su hijo(a). Los materiales nuevos pueden despertar aún más el interés por la escritura.
- **Deje que su hijo(a) le ayude a escribir.**
  Cada vez que usted escriba un mensaje telefónico, una lista de víveres, o una nota, pregunte a su hijo(a) si quiere escribir con usted. Deje que escriba su propia versión, al lado de usted.

  Parent Power by B. Power, © 1999. Portsmouth, NH: Heinemann.

Asking About Groups

Many adults have painful memories of being assigned to the "bluebirds" or "canaries" groups during elementary reading instruction. Grouping for instruction is still an important practice for teachers, because research shows that children learn a lot through small-group discussions with peers and an adult. But the ways groups are assigned, and their purposes, have changed dramatically over the years. Here are some questions you might ask your child or discuss in a conference with the teacher to better understand grouping in the classroom:

- **Do children change groups as the year progresses?**
  Many students, particularly primary-age children, make enormous gains over a short period of time. A group that might be appropriate for one student in October may be the wrong group in March. Ask your child's teacher how group membership shifts as students' needs change.
- **Who works with each group?**
  Parent volunteers and instructional aides can provide valuable support to small groups, in addition to the guidance of the teacher. Ask about roles of different adults in the classroom.
- **Do students have an opportunity to work with many children over the course of the week?**
  If your child needs help with certain reading skills, it's appropriate for the child to be assigned to a small group for instruction targeted at those needs. At the same time, however, all children should have the opportunity to discuss stories and do projects such as a poster or a play about their reading with other children whose strengths and weaknesses are different from their own.
- **What kinds of work do groups do?**
  It could be quick exercises to help develop a certain skill; it might be long-term major projects completed with others. If you ask, you'll have a better sense of how to assist your child.

Preguntar acerca de los grupos

Muchos adultos tienen recuerdos penosos de haber sido asignados a grupos de "azulejos" o "canarios" durante la instrucción de lectura en la escuela primaria. Agrupar con fines de instrucción es todavía una práctica importante para los maestros, ya que las investigaciones demuestran que los niños aprenden mucho mediante conversaciones en pequeños grupos con compañeros y un adulto. Pero la forma en que son asignados los grupos, y sus propósitos, han cambiado drásticamente a través de los años. Aquí presentamos algunas preguntas que usted puede hacer a su hijo(a) o tratar en una conversación con el maestro para entender mejor cómo se forman los grupos en la clase:

- **¿Cambian los niños de grupo en el transcurso del año?**
  Muchos estudiantes, particularmente en edad primaria, avanzan mucho en un corto período de tiempo. Un grupo que podría ser apropiado para un estudiante en octubre, podría no serlo en marzo. Pregunte al maestro de su hijo(a) cómo cambia la participación en los grupos, a medida que cambian las necesidades de los estudiantes.
- **¿Quién trabaja con cada grupo?**
  Los padres voluntarios y los ayudantes de instrucción pueden brindar un apoyo valioso a pequeños grupos, además de la orientación que ofrece el maestro. Pregunte cuáles son las funciones de los adultos en la clase.
- **¿Tienen los estudiantes una oportunidad de trabajar con muchos niños en el transcurso de la semana?**
  Si su hijo(a) necesita ayuda en ciertas habilidades de lectura, resulta adecuado que se le asigne a un grupo pequeño con la instrucción dirigida como objetivo a esas necesidades. Por otra parte, todos los niños deben tener la oportunidad de conversar sobre los cuentos y realizar proyectos tales como un cartel o una obra acerca de su lectura con niños que tengan otros puntos fuertes y débiles.
- **¿Qué tipos de trabajo realizan los grupos?**
  Pueden ser ejercicios rápidos para ayudar a desarrollar una habilidad determinada, tal vez proyectos importantes a largo plazo realizados con otros. Si usted pregunta, entenderá mejor cómo ayudar a su hijo(a).

Adjusting to School

You may notice that the house is a little quiet the first week of school! This is only natural as everyone adjusts to the new routines of schools. Don't expect most children to be very chatty—it's exhausting for anyone to juggle new classrooms, friends, early bedtimes, and earlier wake-up calls! It is an exciting but intense time for children—new friends, new teachers, and new responsibilities can overwhelm even the most confident child. There are small things you can do that your child will appreciate to help them adjust to the new school year:

- **Make sure home routines are very regular.**
  This provides children with a sense of security as they adjust to the new demands of school. Firm bedtimes and consistent routines such as reading together just before lights out will help your child master the new routines away from home much more quickly.
- **Organize that book bag!**
  Now is the time for you to set up a quiet area, time, and ground rules for help with school projects or homework. Read any materials sent home about the school rules and routines carefully, so you can help your child with new responsibilities and rules.
- **Hide a note or two.**
  Write a short note to your child reminding them that you're thinking of them all day long, and then hide it in their lunch or backpack. Your child will love coming across a happy note from home as they are in the midst of adjusting to a new environment.
- **Plan a special event for the weekend.**
  It might include preparing your child's favorite meal, or a last trip to the beach or favorite playground. Celebrate the hard work your child (and you) have done all week adjusting to school by treating yourselves to time together you can both enjoy.

Adaptarse a la escuela

Posiblemente, encontrará la casa un poco tranquila la primera semana de clases. Esto es natural mientras cada uno se adapta a las nuevas rutinas de la escuela. No espere que su hijo(a) le cuente mucho. Resulta agotador para cualquiera enfrentarse a aulas y amigos nuevos, y tener que acostarse y levantarse más temprano. Es una época emocionante pero intensa para los niños. Los nuevos amigos y maestros, y las nuevas responsabilidades pueden agobiar al niño más seguro. Hay pequeñas cosas que usted puede hacer y que su hijo(a) apreciará para adaptarse mejor al nuevo año escolar:

- **Asegúrese de que las rutinas del hogar sean muy metódicas.**
  Esto proporciona a los niños un sentido de seguridad mientras se adaptan a las nuevas exigencias escolares. Un horario fijo para acostarse y rutinas estables, tales como leer juntos antes de apagar las luces, ayudarán a su hijo(a) a adaptarse a las nuevas rutinas fuera del hogar con mayor rapidez.
- **¡Organice esa maleta de libros!**
  Ahora es el momento para que usted establezca un área tranquila, un horario, y reglas de base para las tareas escolares. Lea cualquier material enviado a la casa referente a las reglas y rutinas escolares.
- **Esconda una nota o dos.**
  Escriba una nota corta a su hijo(a) en la que le recuerde que usted está pensando en él o ella durante todo el día, y escóndala luego en su bolsa de merienda o mochila. A su hijo(a) le encantará encontrar una nota feliz de la casa mientras se encuentra en medio de la adaptación a un nuevo medio.
- **Planee un evento especial para el fin de semana.**
  Puede incluir la preparación de la comida favorita de su hijo(a), o un último viaje a la playa o al parque favorito. Celebre el duro trabajo que su hijo(a) (y usted) han realizado durante toda la semana para adaptarse a la escuela proporcionándose un tiempo juntos del cual ambos pueden disfrutar.

Dealing with Concerns

Nothing causes a bigger knot in a parent's stomach than the realization that something is hurting their child. It can be a math program that isn't working for a student, or withdrawal from peers because of playground fights. It's important that you share your concerns if your child seems to be struggling or is having difficulties in school. The teacher may not even be aware of the problem—often the most painful situations involve conflicts with peers, and children are sometimes hesitant to share those problems with a teacher. And if the problem involves the curriculum, it can often be a case of misunderstanding as the curriculum goals are translated by the child to a parent. Here are some steps you can take to make sure concerns are resolved quickly:

- **Write down your concerns first.**
  This isn't writing that you necessarily will want to show a teacher or an administrator, but it will help you focus your concerns. It might also help you diffuse some strong emotions you might be feeling.
- **Be direct.**
  It is often difficult to call a teacher directly—most classrooms do not have telephones. Call the main office and leave a message. As teachers may not have the opportunity to return your call immediately, leave a time it would be best to return the call.
- **Make an appointment if needed.**
  Be sure to let the teacher know why you are asking for the appointment.
- **Keep a positive frame of mind, especially with your child.**
  Remember that you, the teacher, and the child are the partners in your child's education. Often a concern about school is upsetting to both you and your child. Your child's attitude about school is tempered by your feelings and you want your child to have a positive outlook.
- **Be clear about your concerns.**
  An honest approach works best. Let the teacher know your concerns and how they came to be. Though criticism can be painful, teachers much prefer to hear concerns directly than through gossip or another individual. The teacher can offer more information or an explanation that will help the two of you plan a course of action.

Enfrentar las preocupaciones

No hay nada que cause un mayor nudo en el estómago de los padres que darse cuenta de que algo está afectando a su hijo(a). Puede tratarse de un programa de matemáticas que no resulta bueno para un estudiante, o la separación de compañeros debido a peleas en el patio de recreo. Es importante que usted comparta sus preocupaciones si su hijo(a) parece estar atormentado o si tiene dificultades en la escuela. El maestro puede no estar consciente del problema. A veces, las situaciones más penosas son conflictos con compañeros, y los niños a veces no quieren compartir esos problemas con un maestro. Si el problema concierne al currículo, puede tratarse a menudo de un caso de mala interpretación cuando el niño transmite los objetivos del currículo a uno de los padres. A continuación hay algunos pasos que usted puede dar para asegurarse de que las preocupaciones se resuelven con rapidez:

- **Anote primero sus preocupaciones.**
  Esto no es escribir lo que usted necesariamente deseará mostrar a un maestro o administrador, pero ayudará a enfocar sus preocupaciones. Esto también ayuda a difundir las emociones fuertes que usted pueda sentir.
- **Sea directo.**
  A veces resulta difícil llamar a un maestro directamente. La mayoría de las aulas no tienen teléfonos. Llame a la oficina principal y deje un mensaje. Ya que los maestros pueden no tener la oportunidad de devolver su llamada de inmediato, diga la hora en que sería mejor devolver la llamada.
- **Haga una cita si es necesario.**
  Cerciórese de dejar saber al maestro el motivo por el cual usted solicita una cita.
- **Mantenga un estado de ánimo positivo, especialmente con su hijo(a).**
  Recuerde que los tres, usted, el maestro y el niño, tienen que cooperar en la educación de su hijo(a). Una preocupación sobre la escuela puede perturbarlo tanto a usted como a su hijo(a). Las emociones que usted demuestre servirán para moderar las emociones de su hijo(a) y a que mantenga una perspectiva positiva.
- **Exprese claramente sus preocupaciones.**
  La honestidad da mejores resultados. Deje que el maestro conozca sus preocupaciones y cómo surgieron. Aunque las críticas pueden ser desagradables, los maestros prefieren mucho más conocer las preocupaciones directamente que a través de chismes o de otros individuos. El maestro puede ofrecer más información o una explicación que ayude a los dos a planear la forma de proceder.

 Parent Power by B. Power, © 1999. Portsmouth, NH: Heinemann.

Helping Your Child Enter a New School

For a child, enrolling in a new school is exciting—and anxiety-provoking. There are several things you can do to make the change in schools a little easier.

- **Visit the school with your child.**
  Before your child enters the new school, make an appointment to visit the teacher and class-room. Schedule a time when you can introduce your child and yourself to the teacher as well as explore the classroom.
- **Find out about the daily routines.**
  Where do the children line up to come inside in the morning? How is lunch money collected? What is the schedule for gym and art? Is there a dress code? Ask for a student or parent hand-book, if there is one available.
- **Request a tour of the building.**
  Children new to a school are often reluctant to ask about the lost-and-found box or the nurse's station. Tour the school with your child to discover all the important areas, including the main office, bathrooms, library, and gym.
- **Check on school policies.**
  All schools have written policies that guide their procedures. If there isn't a school/parent hand-book, ask about dropping off and picking up children, administering medication, early dismissal, and discipline procedures.
- **Fill out any paperwork you can before that first day.**
  Any paperwork—such as emergency forms or permission slips—that you can fill out beforehand is less for your child to carry back and forth that first day.
- **Find out about supplies.**
  Check to see what supplies your child may need to bring along on that first day. Most schools supply pencils and crayons but other supplies may be the responsibility of the student. Being prepared for that first day helps your child feel secure.
- **Follow the transportation route your child will use to get to school.**
  If your child will travel by bus, check with the school or the bus company about the schedule and pick-up and drop-off points. If your child is a walker, walk the route together and talk about safely walking to school. Point out landmarks that may be helpful in finding the way.

 Parent Power by B. Power, © 1999. Portsmouth, NH: Heinemann.

Ayudar a su hijo(a) a empezar en una nueva escuela

Para un niño, matricularse en una nueva escuela es emocionante. También es algo que provoca ansiedad. Hay varias cosas que usted puede hacer para que el cambio de escuelas sea un poco más fácil.

- **Visite la escuela con su hijo(a).**
  Antes de que su hijo(a) empiece en una nueva escuela, haga una cita para visitar al maestro y el aula. Escoja una hora en la que pueda presentar a su hijo(a) y presentarse usted mismo al maestro a la vez que explora el aula.
- **Averigüe cuáles son las rutinas diarias.**
  ¿Dónde forman la fila los niños para entrar a la escuela por la mañana? ¿Cómo se cobra el dinero del almuerzo? ¿Cuál es el horario de las clases de educación física y de arte? ¿Existen reglas en la forma de vestir? Si la escuela tiene un manual para padres o para estudiantes, pida un ejemplar.
- **Solicite un recorrido por el edificio.**
  Los niños que son nuevos en una escuela a veces rehúsan preguntar dónde se puede recupear los objetos perdidos o dónde está la enfermería. Haga un recorrido por la escuela con su hijo(a) para descubrir todas los puntos importantes, incluyendo la oficina principal, los baños, la biblioteca y el gimnasio.
- **Revise la normas de la escuela.**
  Todas las escuelas tienen normas escritas que definen sus procedimientos. Si la escuela no tiene un manual para los padres, pregunte cómo se dejan y recogen los niños, cómo se administran los medicamentos, cómo se obtienen los permisos para salir temprano y cuáles son los procedimientos disciplinarios.
- **Llene los formularios que pueda antes del primer día.**
  Cualquier papel, tal como los formularios de emergencias o los permisos, que usted pueda llenar de antemano es algo menos que su hijo(a) tendrá que cargar el primer día.
- **Infórmese acerca de los materiales.**
  Averigüe cuáles son los materiales que su hijo(a) debe llevar en ese primer día. La mayoría de las escuelas suministran lápices y creyones, pero los otros materiales pueden ser responsabilidad del estudiante. Prepararse para ese primer día ayudará a su hijo(a) a sentirse seguro.
- **Siga la ruta de transporte que usará su hijo(a) para llegar a la escuela.**
  Si su hijo(a) viaja en autobús, compruebe con la escuela o la compañía de autobuses cuál es el horario y cuáles son los puntos de recogida. Si su hijo(a) va caminando a la escuela, hagan el recorrido juntos y explíquele cuáles son las precauciones que tiene que tomar por el camino a la escuela. Señale los puntos de referencia más útiles para encontrar el camino.

5 Ayudar a su hijo(a) a empezar en una nueva escuela

Parent Power by B. Power, © 1999. Portsmouth, NH: Heinemann.

Television and Learning

Your older child wants to watch MTV. Your younger child wants to watch the Disney Channel. And you would prefer that they turn off the television altogether and find something better to do with their free time. Nothing provokes more concern or guilt in parents than television viewing by their children.

Research shows that many children watch thirty-five hours or more of television per week, and this excessive viewing is linked to many social and academic problems. Child development and education advocacy groups recommend no more than two hours of television per day. The good news is that research shows there are slight academic gains with children who watch small amounts of television daily. The key is to make sure the television choices are thoughtful and planned. Here are some simple steps you can take to ensure that your family makes wise choices when it comes to television viewing.

- **Make homework and chores a priority.**
  Don't allow television viewing in the evening before these tasks are completed.
- **Think about balance.**
  Choose an educational program for your child to watch for every show that's pure entertainment. You and your child can complete this task together using the *TV Guide* or newspaper listings—a fine way to practice some reading skills.
- **Set a limit to television viewing daily, and stick to it.**
  This is sometimes easier to do through a weekly plan. If you go through the schedule on Saturday or Sunday for the entire week, it's not as difficult to say "No!" when your child makes additional requests on a frantic weekday.
- **Replace some television time with other fun time.**
  Even if it's just a ten-minute game of checkers or a quick trip to the playground, your children will gain physically, socially, and academically through more time with you.

La televisión y el aprendizaje

Su hijo(a) mayor desea ver MTV. Su hijo(a) menor desea ver el canal de Disney. Y usted prefiere que ellos apaguen el televisor para siempre y encuentren algo mejor que hacer en su tiempo libre. Nada provoca mayor preocupación o sentido de culpa en los padres que el hecho de que sus hijos(as) vean la televisión.

Las investigaciones revelan que muchos niños miran la televisión treinta y cinco horas o más a la semana, y este exceso está relacionado con muchos problemas sociales y académicos. Los grupos de defensa del desarrollo y educación de los niños recomiendan no más de dos horas de televisión al día. Por el lado positivo tenemos que las investigaciones demuestran cierto beneficio académico en niños que ven poca televisión diariamente. La clave está en pensar y planificar bien los programas televisados. A continuación aparecen varios pasos simples que le ayudarán a tomar buenas decisiones en cuanto a la televisión.

- **Haga que la tarea escolar y los quehaceres domésticos sean una prioridad.**
  No permita mirar la televisión por la noche antes de terminar la tarea.
- **Busque un equilibrio.**
  Escoja un programa educativo para su hijo(a) por cada programa que sea de entretenimiento puro. Usted y su hijo(a) pueden lograr esto juntos usando la *Guía de TV ("TV Guide")* o las programaciones que se publican en los periódicos. Esto es también una buena forma de practicar la lectura.
- **Fije un límite de tiempo para ver la televisión diariamente y cúmplalo.**
  A veces es más fácil lograr esto con un plan semanal. Si usted escoge el sábado o el domingo para escoger la programación de toda la semana, no es tan difícil decirle que no a su hijo(a) cuando le pida ver más televisión un frenético día en medio de la semana.
- **Reemplace parte del tiempo dedicado a la televisión con otra distracción.**
  Aun cuando sólo sea un juego de damas de diez minutos o un corto rato en parque, su hijo(a) recibe un beneficio físico, social y académico, cuando pasa más tiempo con usted.

To View or Not to View: Evaluating Television Programs

It's often easy to judge which television shows are truly educational and worthwhile for children, and which ones are clearly meant only for mature adults. What's harder for most of us is that vast middle ground of television programming that is mostly entertainment, not educational. And these days, the language and content of these shows is getting racier all the time. If your child thinks "PBS" stands for "Pretty Boring Stuff," you might have more of a chore on your hands getting them to view quality programs. Here are some questions to ask yourself when you're deciding whether or not a program is appropriate for your child:

- **Does this program reflect our values?**
  Consider what the program will be teaching your child about life, love, honesty, commitment—or anything else your family values most. Many programs won't promote your values in the same way you do, but if the show works actively against them, it will probably do more harm than good.
- **Can I link this program to my child's learning?**
  If your child loves a particular program, see if there are books tied to it available at the library, bookstore, or through the classroom book club. You may not be crazy about the characters, but if your child adores them, it might be a way to encourage more reading when the television is off.
- **Can the time be better spent doing something else?**
  While it's true that there are often more purposeful activities than watching television, there are also times when viewing is more appropriate than others for children. Television time should come after homework, chores, and family time.
- **What is my bottom line?**
  Trust your instincts in banning certain programs in your home. Every parent knows the perpetual whine of children that "all my friends get to watch this show." Even if a show is off-limits, they still may sneak a peek at a friend's house and hear the plot lines at school or read the show's zingers on classmates' T-shirts. But your child will respect the limits you set, especially if you keep the lines of communication open by talking about what is offensive in a particular program.

Mirar o no mirar: Evaluar los programas de televisión

Es fácil juzgar qué programas de televisión son realmente educativos y valiosos para los niños y cuáles están claramente dirigidos a adultos. Lo que resulta más difícil para la mayoría de nosotros es ese vasto campo medio de la programación de televisión que es fundamentalmente de entretenimiento, no educativo. Y en estos días, el lenguaje y el contenido de esos programas se está haciendo cada vez más picante todo el tiempo. Si su hijo(a) piensa que "PBS" significa "Pretty Boring Stuff" ("Cosas Muy Aburridas"), a usted le puede costar bastante trabajo lograr que vea programas buenos. Estas son algunas preguntas que usted se debe hacer cuando esté decidiendo si un programa es adecuado para su hijo(a):

- **¿Refleja ese programa nuestros valores?**
  Considere lo que ese programa enseñará a su hijo(a) acerca de la vida, el amor, la honradez, las obligaciones, o cualquier otra cosa que su familia valore más. Muchos programas no promueven sus valores de la misma forma en que usted lo hace, pero si el programa actúa activamente en contra de ellos, probablemente hará más daño que bien.
- **¿Puedo vincular este programa al aprendizaje de mi hijo(a)?**
  Si a su hijo(a) le gusta un programa en particular, vea si se pueden obtener libros relacionados con ese programa en la biblioteca, la librería, o el club del libro de la escuela. Puede ser que a usted no le interesen los personajes, pero si le gustan a su hijo(a), esto podría ser un estímulo para que lean más cuando el televisor esté apagado.
- **¿Puede emplearse mejor el tiempo en otra cosa?**
  Si bien es cierto que hay otras actividades positivas, también es cierto que hay momentos en que ver televisión es más adecuado para los niños. El tiempo para ver televisión debe venir después de las tareas escolares, los quehaceres domésticos y el tiempo dedicado a la familia.
- **¿Cuál es mi límite?**
  Confíe en sus instintos al prohibir ciertos programas en su hogar. Cada padre conoce el lamento perpetuo de los niños de que "a todos mis amigos los dejan ver ese programa". Aun cuando el programa esté fuera de los límites establecidos, los niños pueden mirarlo a hurtadillas en casa de un amigo y oír el argumento en la escuela o leer expresiones del programa en las camisetas de los compañeros de clase. Pero su hijo(a) respetará los límites que usted establezca, especialmente si usted mantiene abiertas las líneas de comunicación hablando sobre lo que es ofensivo en un programa particular.

Appreciating Art—Child Style

Seek the wisdom of the ages, but look at the world through the eyes of a child.
–Ron Wild

If it's been awhile since you've visited an art museum or tried to sketch a picture, you owe yourself the treat of looking at art through your child's eyes. You will be surprised and delighted at how much you learn through watching your child enjoy art.

There are many simple things you can do to promote a love of art in your child, as well as rekindle your own enjoyment of paintings, sculpture, and simple sketching:

- **Visit an art museum together.**
  Try to keep visits short. One hour in a museum is plenty for a child. It's fine to see just a small portion of what's being exhibited. Many museums have certain days or hours where there is no charge to view exhibits—call ahead and ask.
- **Take a "sketch walk" together.**
  Buy a new bound journal, or make one with simple paper and staples or tape. Bring along some colored pencils or crayons, and stop every so often to sketch what you see. Fostering an appreciation for detail is a skill your child will use throughout their learning in school.
- **Stock up on low-cost art supplies.**
  Many children prefer markers to crayons, or crayons to colored pencils. If you find out what your child likes, you can keep an eye out for sales on their favorite materials. New interest in art is sparked when new supplies or paper is brought out.
- **Ask about drawings your child brings home from school.**
  If you ask your child about and compliment their development of drawing abilities, you are actually helping them develop their thinking abilities. Many children think more with "pictures in their heads" rather than words—by discussing their drawing, you help them think through what they are learning in new ways.

If you're not skilled as an artist, don't worry. Your child will think you are a fantastic sketcher, and their praise will be genuine. Children love to have partners as they sketch, draw, and color. And you will quickly discover that your art time together creates some very pleasurable memories of childhood.

   Parent Power by B. Power, © 1999. Portsmouth, NH: Heinemann.

Apreciar el arte al estilo del niño

Busque la sabiduría de la época, pero mire el mundo a través de los ojos de un niño.
—Ron Wild

Si hace mucho tiempo desde que usted visitó un museo de arte o trató de esbozar una pintura, se merece el placer de contemplar el arte a través de los ojos de su hijo(a). Usted se sorprenderá y se deleitará al saber lo mucho que usted aprende al ver a su hijo(a) disfrutar del arte.

Hay muchas cosas simples que usted puede hacer para promover el amor al arte en su hijo(a), al igual que despertar su propio disfrute de las pinturas, las esculturas y los dibujos:

- **Visiten un museo de arte juntos.**
  Trate de mantener las visitas cortas. Una hora en un museo es suficiente para un niño. Está bien ver solamente una pequeña parte de lo que se está exhibiendo. Muchos museos no cobran la entrada ciertos días o a ciertas horas. Llame y pregunte.
- **Den un paseo juntos para dibujar.**
  Compre un cuaderno de dibujo, o haga uno con hojas de papel planco y grápelas o péguelas con cinta adhesiva. Lleve algunos lápices o creyones de colores, y deténganse a menudo para dibujar de lo que ven. Anime a su hijo(a) a percibir detalles, una habilidad que le será siempre útil en la escuela.
- **Mantenga un surtido de materiales de arte de bajo costo.**
  Muchos niños prefieren marcadores en lugar de creyones, o creyones en lugar de lápices de colores. Averigüe lo que le gusta a su hijo(a), y aproveche cuando rebajen los precios de sus materiales favoritos. Los materiales y papeles nuevos despertarán el interés de su hijo(a) por dibujar.
- **Haga preguntas a su hijo(a) sobre los dibujos que trae a la casa de la escuela.**
  Al preguntarle a su hijo(a) acerca de sus dibujos y felicitarlo por sus logros, realmente lo estará ayudando a desarrollar sus capacidad de pensar. Muchos niños piensan más con imágenes mentales que con palabras. Al hablar sobre su dibujo, usted ayuda a su hijo(a) a pensar de otra manera acerca de lo que está aprendiendo.

Si usted no tiene habilidades como artista, no se preocupe. Su hijo(a) pensará que usted hace dibujos maravillosos, y su elogio será genuino. A los niños les encanta tener compañeros cuando hacen dibujos o colorean y usted descubrirá rápidamente que el tiempo que dediquen juntos al arte crea algunos recuerdos muy placenteros de la niñez.

 Parent Power by B. Power, © 1999. Portsmouth, NH: Heinemann.

Coping with Conflict

It goes without saying that you should never have more children than you have car windows.

—Erma Bombeck

Any time children are together—at school or at home—there inevitably will be conflicts. Teachers have a few options—they can buy thirty sets of everything and rent a warehouse for storing materials, or they can try to teach kids to share. Parents can stock up on ace bandages for wounds and earplugs to block out screaming—or they can help children learn how to resolve differences without fighting.

Seriously, teachers and parents share the same goal when it comes to dealing with children's conflicts. We all want children to learn how to resolve differences on their own, in mature and fair ways that show respect for all. As you deal with children who are in conflict with others, keep asking them these questions:

- **What was your part in the conflict?**
  Sometimes it truly is the other child's fault, but usually there are at least two sides to the conflict. By helping your child see their role in the disagreement, you help them take responsibility for resolving the problem.
- **What options are there for solving this problem?**
  By helping your child see that there are often many possibilities for resolving differences, you will build (over time) their abilities as problem solvers in many different situations.
- **How do you think the other child views this situation?**
  Helping your child see the point of view of others is a critical aspect of development. Becoming more mature is a process of being able to step more and more into the shoes and viewpoints of others.

You probably won't want to throw out your supplies of Band-Aids anytime soon. But using these questions to help your child think about conflicts with others may help you see slow progress toward the goal of enabling your child to resolve differences with others without adult intervention.

Hacer frente a los conflictos

No hace falta decir que usted no debe tener más niños que ventanillas en el carro.
—Erma Bombeck

Cada vez que los niños están juntos, ya sea en la escuela o en la casa, inevitablemente habrá conflictos. Los maestros tienen unas pocas opciones: pueden comprar treinta juegos de todo y alquilar un almacén para guardar tantos materiales, o pueden tratar de enseñar a los niños a compartir. Los padres pueden almacenar vendas para heridas y orejeras para bloquear los gritos, o bien, pueden ayudar a los niños a aprender cómo resolver las diferencias sin pelear.

Seriamente, los maestros y los padres comparten el mismo objetivo al enfrentar los conflictos de los niños. Todos queremos que los niños aprendan cómo resolver las diferencias a su manera, de una forma madura y justa y que muestre respeto para todos. Cuando usted trata con niños que están en conflicto, hágales estas preguntas:

- **¿Cuál es tu parte en el conflicto?**
  A veces realmente la culpa es del otro niño, pero generalmente hay al menos dos versiones en el conflicto. Al ayudar a su hijo(a) a ver su participación en el desacuerdo, usted lo ayuda a asumir la responsabilidad de resolver el problema.
- **¿Qué opciones existen para resolver este problema?**
  Al ayudar a su hijo(a) a ver que pueden existir muchas posibilidades de resolver diferencias, usted contribuirá a que desarrolle (en el transcurso del tiempo) su capacidad como individuo que resuelve problemas en situaciones muy diferentes.
- **¿Cómo piensas que el otro niño ve la situación?**
  Ayudar a su hijo(a) a ver el punto de vista de los otros es un aspecto crítico del desarrollo. Madurar es un proceso que implica ser capaz de participar cada vez más en los problemas de los otros y considerar sus puntos de vista.

Probablemente no conviene que usted se deshaga completamente de todas las vendas que tiene en el botiquín, pero estas preguntas ayudarán a su hijo(a) a pensar sobre los conflictos con los otros. Usted verá cómo su hijo(a) progresa lentamente, hasta el día en que pueda resolver las diferencias con otros niños sin la intervención de los adultos.

Building a Low-Cost Library of Books

Reading to your child is essential for their success in school. But just as important for reading success is having regular access to books in the home. Your child's tastes and abilities as a reader will change rapidly during the elementary years. While the cost of new hardcover books can be prohibitively expensive, there are many low-cost options for building a home library, including book clubs and garage sales. To make the most of these low-cost opportunities, make sure you:

- **Know what your child likes.**
  Children are into series—first favorite authors, and then favorite types of books. If your child loves the "Arthur" series by Marc Brown or "Berenstain Bears" books, you can look for these at garage sales or book exchanges at school.
- **Let your child choose.**
  Your child may choose a book that seems far too simple (or complex) for their reading level. That's all right—allowing them to make choices teaches them responsibility, and they might surprise you with how much they can read or enjoy a book you wouldn't have picked.
- **Like new is best.**
  At pennies per copy, it's sometimes tempting to purchase well-worn books with decrepit covers at garage or rummage sales. Don't make that mistake—no self-respecting kid will choose to read a book that looks like it's been run over by a truck. If the books aren't in like-new condition, chances are they won't be read at home.
- **Exchange with friends.**
  Friends who have children older or younger than yours might be open to a book exchange or a loan of books appropriate for your child.

You will be amazed at how quickly you can build a home library with used books, at a fraction of the cost of purchasing new ones.

Crear una biblioteca de libros de bajo costo

Leer resulta esencial para el éxito de su hijo en la escuela. Pero para el éxito en la lectura es igualmente importante tener acceso a libros en la casa. Los gustos y habilidades de su hijo(a) como lector cambiarán rápidamente durante los años de la enseñanza primaria. Si bien el costo de los libros nuevos puede ser prohibitivamente elevado, existen muchas opciones de bajo costo para crear una biblioteca en el hogar, incluyendo clubs del libro y ventas de libros de uso. Para aprovechar al máximo esas oportunidades de bajo costo, asegúrese de:

- **Saber lo que le gusta a su hijo(a).**
  A los niños les gustan las series. Primero pueden tener autores favoritos y después preferir ciertos tipos de libros. Si a su hijo(a) le gusta la serie "Arthur" de Marc Brown o los libros "Berenstain Bears", usted puede buscarlos en las ventas de segunda o conseguirlos mediante intercambios de libros en la escuela.
- **Dejar que su hijo(a) escoja.**
  Su hijo(a) puede escoger un libro que parezca muy simple (o complejo) para su nivel de lectura. Eso está bien, el hecho de dejar que decida por su cuenta le enseña el sentido de responsabilidad. Su hijo(a) puede sorprenderlo con lo mucho que puede leer o disfrutar de un libro que usted no había escogido.
- **Recordar que entre más nuevo esté el libro, mejor.**
  A centavos por cada ejemplar, a veces resulta tentador comprar libros bien deteriorados con cubiertas estropeadas en ventas de segunda mano. No cometa ese error. Ningún niño que se respete a sí mismo va a escoger para leer un libro que parece que ha sido aplastado por un camión. Si los libros no están en una condición que parezcan nuevos, lo más probable es que se queden sin leer.
- **Hacer intercambios con amigos.**
  Amigos que tienen hijos(as) mayores o menores que los suyos pueden estar dispuestos a intercambiar libros o a prestar libros adecuados para su hijo(a).

Usted se sorprenderá de la rapidez con que puede crear una biblioteca en el hogar con libros usados, a una fracción del costo de comprarlos nuevos.

Children's Hobbies

Watch your child as they are involved in a favorite hobby, and you will be amazed at the learning going on. Some children can rattle off the batting averages of dozens of baseball players; others can recount in minute detail the differences between a basking and a great white shark. All that attention to detail and memorization enhances brain development and helps children acquire essential skills for learning in school.

It's normal and natural for children to develop passionate interests. Humans crave deep knowledge about a small number of things. The way a child develops and explores an interest can give you insight into the kind of learner they are, and what their strengths are as a learner. Often this begins with a desire to collect something—bugs, bottle caps, or a certain type of doll or action figure. As a parent, you have to endure the pop culture fads that children will latch onto. But you can encourage more enduring collections and interests, and use them to teach your child important concepts.

For example, a child who is fascinated by bugs will quickly learn some of the different classification systems for insects. This sorting and close observation serves children well when they participate in science experiments in school. A child who loves ballerinas can read books about famous ballerinas. In this way, a student not only develops reading skills but learns of the patience, persistence, and hard work that are necessary to be a fine artist.

There are obviously a few interests that should concern any parent, like an obsession with guns, violence, or hurting animals. If you're concerned about a particular interest of your child, talk about it with the teacher. But with appropriate interests, you may want to encourage your child to expand, not limit, their thinking about the subject. Help them begin a collection. Go to a museum to see a particularly large display of their favorite things. Attend a ball game, concert, or performance to see masters of their hobby at work. Talk to them about your own childhood hobbies. As you share these interests together, you'll build new bonds.

Pasatiempos de los niños

Mire a su hijo(a) mientras se dedica a su pasatiempo favorito, y usted se asombrará de lo que aprende. Algunos niños enumeran rápidamente los promedios de bateo de docenas de jugadores de pelota; otros pueden describir en los mínimos detalles las diferencias entre un tiburón toro y un gran tiburón blanco. Toda esa atención puesta en el detalle y la memorización fortalece el desarrollo de la mente y ayuda a que los niños adquieran las habilidades esenciales para aprender en la escuela.

Es natural que los niños desarrollen intereses apasionados. Los seres humanos anhelan un conocimiento profundo sobre un número pequeño de cosas. La manera en que un niño desarrolla y explora un interés le puede dar una visión de la clase de alumno que es, y de cuáles son sus fuerzas como alumno. A menudo esto comienza con un deseo de coleccionar algo: insectos, tapas de botella, o cierto tipo de muñecas o juguetes mecánicos. Como padre, usted tiene que soportar las modas populares a las que se aficionan los niños. Pero usted puede alentar colecciones e intereses más tolerables, y usarlos para enseñar a su hijo(a) conceptos importantes.

Por ejemplo, un niño al que le fascinen los insectos aprenderá rápidamente algunos de los diferentes sistemas de clasificación de los insectos. Esta clasificación y observación minuciosa es de gran utilidad a los niños cuando participan en experimentos científicos en la escuela. Un niño a quien le gusten las bailarinas de ballet puede leer libros acerca de bailarinas famosas. De esta forma, su hijo(a) no sólo desarrollará hábitos de lectura, sino que también aprenderá el valor de la paciencia, la persistencia y el trabajo arduo, que exige la profesión de artista.

Obviamente hay algunos intereses que deben preocupar a cualquier padre, como una obsesión por los revólveres, la violencia o hacer daño a los animales. Si usted está preocupado por un interés particular de su hijo(a), consúltelo con el maestro. Pero cuando se trata de intereses adecuados, usted quizás quiera estimular a su hijo(a) a que aumente, y no limite, su pensamiento acerca del tema. Ayúdelo a comenzar una colección. Vaya a un museo a ver una exhibición amplia de sus cosas favoritas. Asista a un juego de pelota, un concierto, o una actuación en la que vea trabajar a los expertos de su pasatiempo. Háblele acerca de sus propios pasatiempos en su niñez. En la medida en que usted comparta esos intereses con él o ella, usted creará nuevos vínculos.

 Parent Power by B. Power, © 1999. Portsmouth, NH: Heinemann.

Understanding Phonics

It is amazing how much controversy the issue of teaching phonics in reading has caused over the past few years. "Phonics" are simply the sounds different letters make individually or in combination with other letters. Linguists, professionals who spend all their time studying language and how it changes over time, have developed some complicated distinctions between these different sounds. But most teachers and children do not need to understand the difference between a "diphthong" or "digraph" in order to learn the phonics they need to read. The same is true for parents—you don't need to have a great deal of knowledge of phonics rules to understand how phonics are being taught in the classroom. Here are some ways to build your understanding of the teacher's phonics instruction program:

- **Ask for an explanation of how phonics is taught.**
  You might be surprised at the many ways students are encouraged to test out and use their understanding of sounds. For example, misspelled words in writing are used by many teachers to diagnose what sounds children know—and what sounds they still need to work with over time.
- **Know there is a sequence of phonics learning.**
  Though all children learn at their own pace, there is a regular order to learning the different sounds in the English language. Different vowel combinations are much more complex, and take more time. This is because the difference in vowel sounds can be subtle, or nonexistent.
- **Encourage your child to write at home.**
  Children will pick up consonant sounds first. Early writing often involves putting down first consonant sounds in words, with final and middle consonant sounds coming later. Ask what sounds your child hears in different words as they read to you or write. If they are early in the process, nudge them toward writing consonant sounds. If they seem to be mastering consonants, encourage attempts at vowel sounds.
- **Encourage your child to read at home.**
  Research shows that children master dozens of phonetic rules for vowels most readily by reading lots of materials. Through exposure to umpteen examples of different vowels in print, the brain sifts, sorts, and begins to recognize phonics patterns that are too complex to be taught directly.

Entender la fonética

Es sorprendente saber cuánta controversia ha causado en los últimos años el problema de la enseñanza de la fonética en la lectura. El sistema de enseñanza conocido en inglés como "Phonics" trata simplemente de los sonidos que tienen las letras individualmente, o en combinación con otras letras. Los lingüistas, profesionales que dedican todo su tiempo a estudiar el lenguaje y cómo el mismo cambia a través del tiempo, han desarrollado algunas distinciones complicadas entre esos sonidos. Pero la mayor parte de los maestros y niños no necesitan entender la diferencia entre un "diptongo" y un "digrafo" para aprender la fonética que necesitan leer. Lo mismo es cierto para los padres: usted no necesita tener un gran conocimiento de las reglas de fonética para entender cómo se enseña la fonética en la clase. Estas son algunas formas de aprender cómo funciona el programa de instrucción de fonética del maestro:

- **Pida una explicación de cómo se enseña la fonética.**
  Usted puede sorprenderse de las muchas formas en que se anima a los estudiantes a practicar y usar su conocimiento de los sonidos. Por ejemplo, muchos maestros usan las palabras mal deletreadas en la escritura para diagnosticar qué sonidos conocen los niños, y con cuáles necesitan todavía practicar.
- **Conozca que existe una secuencia en el aprendizaje de la fonética.**
  Aunque todos los niños aprenden a su propio ritmo, existe un orden establecido para aprender los diferentes sonidos en el idioma inglés. Las diferentes combinaciones de vocales son mucho más complejas, y toman más tiempo. Esto se debe a que puede haber diferencias muy sutiles entre las vocales.
- **Aliente a su hijo(a) a escribir en la casa.**
  Los niños captarán primero los sonidos de las consonantes. La escritura temprana a menudo implica poner los sonidos de las primeras consonantes en las palabras y después los sonidos de las consonantes intermedias y finales. Pregunte qué sonidos oye su hijo(a) en las diferentes palabras cuando lee para usted o cuando escribe. Si está adelantado en el proceso, adviértale que debe escribir los sonidos de las consonantes. Si parece que está dominando las consonantes, anímelo a intentar con los sonidos de las vocales.
- **Estimule a su hijo(a) a leer en la casa.**
  Las investigaciones revelan que los niños dominan docenas de reglas fonéticas para las vocales con bastante facilidad mediante la lectura de muchos materiales. Mediante la exposición a muchísimos ejemplos de diferentes vocales impresas, el cerebro examina, clasifica y comienza a reconocer patrones fonéticos que serían muy complejos de enseñarse directamente.

Getting Involved in Your Child's Classroom

A school is a community, built from the families of the children who attend. Parents are welcome to visit and to get involved in the classroom. Even if you work full-time, there are small ways that you can assist in your child's classroom:

- **Volunteer to help in the classroom at regular times.**
  Many parents can't make this commitment, and some teachers prefer to limit the number of regular classroom helpers. But nothing gives you a better sense of your child's learning than to be a part of the classroom every week or month.
- **Volunteer to assist from home.**
  There may be tasks that you can complete at home to help the classroom run smoothly. These might include some research into units on the Internet, word-processing student work for class "publications," or assembling materials for craft projects.
- **Offer to assist with field trips.**
  Often these are scheduled well in advance of the event, which can allow some parents to juggle their commitments and participate. A field trip is an exciting activity for your child. Many times this involves hands-on activities, and an extra pair of supervising hands is often appreciated.
- **Make a list of special skills or interests you have, and volunteer to share these with the class.**
  The class might have a February unit on sharks that dovetails nicely with your collection of shark photos and teeth; your interest in garden herbs might connect with a garden-growing project scheduled for spring. When this information is given early in the fall, planning for the entire year is much easier.
- **Attend open houses and parent-teacher conferences.**
  Open house at your child's school is a time for them to display their work and show you where they spend the majority of their day.

Participar en la clase de su hijo(a)

Una escuela es una comunidad formada por las familias de los niños que asisten a la misma. Los padres son bienvenidos a visitar y participar en la clase. Aun cuando usted trabaje a tiempo completo, existen formas sencillas en las que usted puede ayudar en la clase de su hijo(a).

- **Ofrézcase como voluntario para ayudar en la clase en horarios fijos.**
  Muchos padres no pueden hacer este compromiso, y algunos maestros prefieren limitar el número de personas que ayudan en la clase de forma fija. Pero no hay nada que le proporcione una mejor visión del aprendizaje de su hijo que participar en la clase cada semana o cada mes.
- **Ofrézcase como voluntario para ayudar desde la casa.**
  Pueden existir tareas que usted podría realizar en la casa para ayudar a que la clase se desenvuelva sin dificultad. Estas pueden incluir algunas investigaciones sobre las unidades en Internet, realizar trabajos estudiantiles en la computadora con el fin de presentarlos como "publicaciones" de la clase, o reunir materiales para proyectos de artesanía.
- **Ofrézcase para ayudar en las excursiones.**
  A menudo éstas se programan con anticipación al evento, lo que permite a algunos padres poder organizar sus compromisos y participar. Una excursión es una actividad emocionante para su hijo(a). Muchas veces esto implica experimentación directa. El maestro también agradecerá un par de manos adicionales que supervisen.
- **Haga una lista de habilidades o intereses especiales que usted tiene, y ofrézcase como voluntario para compartirlos con la clase.**
  La clase puede tener en febrero una unidad sobre tiburones que se ajusta bien a su colección de fotos y dientes de tiburones; su interés por las hierbas del jardín puede relacionarse con un proyecto de cultivo de jardines programado para la primavera. Cuando se brinda esta información temprano en el otoño, es mucho más fácil hacer planes para todo el año.
- **Asista a los "open houses" (días de visita) y a conferencias de padres y maestros.**
  La apertura de la escuela de su hijo(a) es un momento para que ellos muestren su trabajo y le enseñen dónde pasan la mayor parte del día.

 Parent Power by B. Power, © 1999. Portsmouth, NH: Heinemann.

Reading Around the House

All parents know it's important to read to their children—public service announcements on the radio and television remind us all the time about the value of home reading. While those ten or fifteen minutes of reading to your child are golden, there are also other things you can do around the house to promote a love of reading, even when you and your child don't have your heads bent together over a book:

- **Provide a special place to store books and a comfortable reading spot.**
  A bookshelf, table by the bedside with a warm light, or bean bag in the family room with a small stand of books beside it are inviting for any young reader.
- **Display your own collection of books with pride.**
  Sharing with your child what books or magazines you're reading, along with the reasons they give you pleasure, is the best model for the joys of reading you can offer.
- **Bring a variety of books and reading materials into your home.**
  Books, newspapers, and magazines offer a variety that ensures there is never a slump in home reading activity.
- **Talk about books at the dinner table.**
  If you share what you are reading first, you're more likely to get a response from your child.
- **Schedule a quiet reading time each night.**
  Turn off the television for fifteen minutes or more so that everyone has a chance to read books quietly. If you observe your children out of the corner of your eye, you'll get a sense of what books they are enjoying the most. You can also see if the reading nook you've set up is comfortable, or if adjustments need to be made.

Leer en la casa

Todos los padres saben que es importante leer a sus hijos(as). Los anuncios de servicio público en la radio y la televisión nos recuerdan todo el tiempo el valor de la lectura en el hogar. Si bien esos diez o quince minutos de lectura a su hijo(a) son muy valiosos, hay también otras cosas que usted puede hacer en la casa para inculcar el amor por la lectura, aun cuando usted y su hijo(a) estén todo el tiempo leyendo.

- **Proporcione un lugar especial para guardar los libros y un rincón agradable para leer.**
  Un estante de libros, una mesa junto a la cama con una luz apropiada, o una silla o cojines en la sala, con un pequeño librero al lado, son medios que invitan a cualquier lector joven.
- **Exhiba con orgullo su propia colección de libros.**
  Compartir con su hijo(a) los libros o revistas que usted está leyendo, junto con los motivos por los que le causan deleite, es el mejor ejemplo que usted puede ofrecer para despertar el amor por la lectura.
- **Traiga a su casa una variedad de libros y materiales de lectura.**
  Los libros, periódicos y revistas ofrecen una variedad que aseguran que nunca haya un vacío en la actividad de lectura en el hogar.
- **Hable sobre libros durante la cena.**
  Si usted comparte lo que está leyendo primero, es más probable que obtenga una respuesta de su hijo(a).
- **Programe un horario de lectura tranquilo cada noche.**
  Apague la televisión durante quince minutos o más de manera que todos tengan la oportunidad de leer libros calladamente. Si usted observa a su hijo(a) con el rabillo del ojo, tendrá una idea de cuáles son los libros que disfruta más. Usted también puede ver si el rincón de lectura que usted ha creado resulta cómodo, o si hace falta hacer ajustes.

Alternatives to Grades

When most of us were students, grades were the only way teachers judged the ability of students. Whether the grade was a *C* or an *85,* we learned at a very early age that our achievements would be distilled down into a letter or number.

Things have changed in schools. While grades are still common in many classrooms, there are a variety of other ways that children are evaluated. Here is a sampling of the alternatives to grades that you might see as your child moves through the elementary grades:

- **Narratives**
  A narrative is a report about your child's progress created from the teacher's notes and observations. The narrative might be two or three paragraphs long, or as lengthy as a few pages.
- **Learning Logs**
  These are notes taken by children about their own learning in a specific area (such as reading or science). Often there are responses from the teacher that encourage students to elaborate on what they are learning or to do further reflection about specific activities or assignments.
- **School-Home Notebooks (or Journals)**
  These are similar to a learning log, but they have the added benefit of responses from both teachers and parents. They are sent home periodically, and families are invited to respond.
- **Rubrics**
  A rubric is a chart or grid that lists certain goals of any project or curricular area, with the students and teachers responsible for checking off which goals were or weren't achieved.
- **Checklists**
  Similar to a rubric, checklists note the key attributes of any learning in a particular subject area, in order to help students or teachers chart progress.
- **Portfolios**
  A portfolio is a collection of your child's work that might include some reflection by the student and teacher about what was learned over time. The advantage of a portfolio is that it shows changes in growth and learning through the student's own work.

If you're confused by any aspect of how your child is evaluated, just ask for an explanation. Everything done to assess your child—from grades to portfolios—is designed to give you a better sense of what your child knows and still needs to learn.

Alternativas a las calificaciones

Cuando la mayoría de nosotros éramos estudiantes, las calificaciones, o notas, eran la única forma en que los maestros juzgaban la habilidad de los estudiantes. Si la calificación era una *C* o un *85*, aprendíamos a una edad muy temprana que nuestros logros se reflejarían en una letra o cifra.

Las cosas han cambiado en las escuelas. Aunque las notas son todavía comunes en muchas clases, existen muchas otras formas de evaluar a los niños. Aquí damos una muestra de otros tipos de calificaciones que quizás usted encuentre mientras su hijo cursa la escuela primaria.

- **Narraciones**
  Una narración es un informe acerca del progreso de su hijo(a) creado a partir de las notas y observaciones del maestro. La narración puede tener dos o tres párrafos, o varias páginas.
- **Cuadernos de aprendizaje**
  Estos están compuestos de notas tomadas por niños acerca de su propio aprendizaje en un área específica (como lectura o las ciencias). Es común que contengan comentarios del maestro que alientan a los estudiantes a trabajar sobre lo que están aprendiendo o a hacer más reflexiones sobre actividades o tareas específicas.
- **Libretas (o diarios) de la escuela y la casa**
  Estas son similares a un cuaderno de aprendizaje, pero tienen además la ventaja de contener tanto los comentarios del maestro como los comentarios de los padres. Se envían a la casa periódicamente, y se invita a las familias a que respondan.
- **Rúbricas**
  Una rúbrica es una tabla o gráfico que enumera ciertas metas de cualquier proyecto o asignatura del currículo, con los estudiantes y maestros responsables de evaluar cuáles fueran las metas que se alcanzaron y cuáles no.
- **Listas de verificación**
  En forma similar a una rúbrica, las listas de verificación anotan los atributos clave de cualquier aprendizaje sobre un tema específico, con el fin de ayudar a los estudiantes o maestros a llevar un registro del progreso.
- **Carpetas**
  En una carpeta se reúne el trabajo de su hijo(a) y puede incluir algunas reflexiones hechas por el estudiante y el maestro acerca de lo que aprendió en el transcurso del tiempo. La ventaja de la carpeta es que muestra los cambios y el desarrollo del aprendizaje a través del propio trabajo del estudiante.

Si usted está confundido en cuanto a algún aspecto de cómo se evalúa a su hijo(a), simplemente pida una explicación. Cualquier cosa que se haga para evaluar a su hijo —desde las notas hasta las carpetas— ha sido diseñada para darle una mejor visión de los conocimientos de su hijo(a) y de lo que necesita aprender todavía.

 Parent Power by B. Power, © 1999. Portsmouth, NH: Heinemann.

Standardized Tests, Part 1

When people go to get a driver's license, they take a standardized test that ensures that they know basic laws and rules of the road. It's essential that any potential driver pass this written test before being given a road test. But no one is handed a driver's license after getting a few multiple-choice questions right. The written test is merely the first step in seeing if someone is ready to demonstrate more complex skills.

The same principle holds with standardized tests in schools. They are one way of assessing knowledge, among many different kinds of evaluation. There are some things you can do to understand these tests better, and to help your child do their best on them:

- **Ask if the test is norm-referenced or criterion-referenced.**
  Norm-referenced tests compare test takers to each other; criterion-referenced tests measure whether or not test takers have mastered specific skills or content. For example, the written portion of the driver's test is criterion-referenced. Test takers are expected to know certain rules and laws. If it was norm-referenced, the test would be designed to ensure that a significant number of test takers failed. Norm-referenced tests often contain odd or difficult questions that aren't designed to test knowledge as much as to sort children into high, middle, and low categories.
- **Ask what the purpose of the test is.**
  Many standardized tests aren't designed to measure individual achievement—they are only meant to consider success or failure across large groups of students.
- **Ask about the school's scores over time, and how they have changed.**
  Looking at scores in isolation can't tell anyone much about school achievement. Ask what the trends are. Have the scores gone up over the past few years? Have they gone down? How is the school using the information the tests provide?

Understanding the purpose of standardized tests can help you and your child keep them in perspective, as one small piece in the puzzle of understanding the school assessment system.

Pruebas estandarizadas, Parte 1

Cuando una persona solicita su licencia de conducir, tiene que pasar una prueba estandarizada para demostrar que conoce las leyes y reglas básicas del tráfico. Es esencial que cualquier chofer potencial pase esta prueba escrita antes de que se le someta a una prueba en la calle. Pero a nadie se le entrega una licencia de conducir después de contestar bien unas cuantas preguntas de seleccion múltiple. La prueba escrita es simplemente el primer paso para determinar si una persona está preparada para demostrar habilidades más complejas.

El mismo principio se cumple con las pruebas estandarizadas en las escuelas. Hay una forma de evaluar el conocimiento, entre muy diferentes clases de evaluación. Hay algunas cosas que usted puede hacer para comprender mejor esas pruebas y para ayudar a que su hijo realice su mayor esfuerzo y obtenga mejor resultado en ellas:

- **Pregunte si la prueba es referida a normas o referida a criterios.**
  Las pruebas referidas a normas comparan entre sí a los que toman las pruebas; las pruebas referidas a criterios miden si los que toman las pruebas dominan habilidades o contenidos específicos. Por ejemplo, la parte escrita de la prueba del chofer es referida a criterios. Se espera que los que toman la prueba conozcan ciertas reglas y leyes. Si fuera una prueba referida a normas, la misma se diseñaría para asegurar que un número significativo de personas que toman la prueba fallen. Las pruebas referidas a normas por lo general contienen preguntas extrañas o difíciles que no están diseñadas para comprobar el conocimiento, sino más bien para clasificar a los niños en categorías altas, intermedias o bajas.
- **Pregunte cuál es el propósito de la prueba.**
  Muchas pruebas estandarizadas no están diseñadas para medir los logros individuales. Sólo están destinadas a considerar el éxito o el fracaso en grupos grandes de estudiantes.
- **Pregunte cuáles son las calificaciones en toda la escuela y cómo han evolucionado con el tiempo.**
  Las calificaciones aisladas pueden no decir mucho acerca de los logros escolares. Pregunte cuáles son las tendencias en toda la escuela. ¿Han subido las calificaciones en los últimos años? ¿Han bajado? ¿Cómo usa la escuela la información que proporciona la prueba?

Comprender el propósito de las pruebas estandarizadas puede ayudarlo a usted y a su hijo a mantener las calificaciones en perspectiva, como una pequeña pieza en el rompecabezas del conocimiento del sistema de evaluación escolar.

 Parent Power by B. Power, © 1999. Portsmouth, NH: Heinemann.

Standardized Tests, Part 2

Few people of any age enjoy the stress of taking a timed test. The environment for taking standardized tests is often pressure-filled, because the stakes can be high for individual students and schools. If you fail your driver's test, only you will know. But if a school does poorly on a standardized test, the scores are often published in the local newspaper!

Like the written component of the driving test, standardized tests are only one way of many used to understand what children are learning. High or low scores on these tests alone for any child shouldn't be cause for celebration or alarm—teachers will provide more complex measures of your child's learning in the classroom that will give you a better sense of your child's needs and strengths as a learner. To help your child prepare for a test, and to understand the test better yourself, you can:

- **Ask to see a sample copy of the test.**
  While teachers can't show the actual test that will be used, they often have old test copies or sample questions. Whether you view a sample copy of the test before or after your child takes it, it will help you understand what the exam is designed to measure.
- **Find out when the test is being given, and make sure your child has some extra rest and a good breakfast the morning before.**
  This ensures that your child has the energy they need to do their best.
- **If your child seems particularly concerned about upcoming standardized tests, talk with the teacher.**
  There may be additional ways you can help your child relax and do their best on these tests.

We often overemphasize the importance of standardized tests in our society. Try to avoid that mistake in your home. Make sure your child knows you appreciate their many achievements in and out of school, regardless of their scores on standardized tests. After all, how many adults would like their attractiveness evaluated on the basis of their driver's license photo alone? While standardized tests can provide useful information to teachers and parents, they are only a snapshot of what a child can do on a particular day.

Pruebas estandarizadas, Parte 2

A pocas personas de cualquier edad les gusta el estrés de tomar una prueba cronometrada. El medio que rodea las pruebas estandarizadas está lleno de presión, ya que los riesgos pueden ser altos para los estudiantes y las escuelas. Si usted falla en su prueba de chofer, sólo usted lo sabrá. Pero si todos los estudiantes de una escuela reciben calificaciones bajas en una prueba estandarizada, los resultados por lo general se publican en el periódico local.

Al igual que el componente escrito de la prueba de conducción, las pruebas estandarizadas constituyen sólo una forma de las muchas que se usan para comprender lo que los niños están aprendiendo. Las calificaciones altas o bajas en estas pruebas solas obtenidas por cualquier niño no deben ser motivo de celebración o alarma. Los maestros brindarán evaluaciones más complejas del aprendizaje de su hijo(a) en la clase, lo cual le dará una mejor visión de las necesidades de su hijo(a) y de las fuerzas con que cuenta para aprender. Para ayudar a preparar a su hijo(a) para una prueba, y para que usted mismo pueda comprender mejor la prueba, usted puede:

- **Pedir ver una copia de muestra de la prueba.**
  Aunque los maestros no pueden enseñar la prueba verdadera que se usará, a veces tienen copias de pruebas viejas o preguntas de muestra. Si usted mira una copia de muestra de la prueba antes o después de que su hijo(a) la tome, eso lo ayudará a comprender qué mide el examen.
- **Averigüe cuándo se realizará la prueba y asegúrese de que su hijo(a) tenga un descanso adicional y un buen desayuno la mañana del día en que tomará la prueba.**
  Esto asegura que su hijo(a) tenga la energía que necesita para rendir el máximo.
- **Si su hijo parece estar muy preocupado acerca de las pruebas estandarizadas, hable con el maestro.**
  Pueden existir formas adicionales de ayudar a que su hijo se sienta relajado y rinda al máximo en esas pruebas.

A veces hacemos un hincapié excesivo en la importancia de las pruebas estandarizadas en nuestra sociedad. Trate de evitar ese error en su casa. Cerciórese de que su hijo(a) sepa que usted aprecia sus muchos logros dentro y fuera de la escuela, independientemente de sus calificaciones en las pruebas estandarizadas. Después de todo, ¿les gustaría acaso a muchos adultos que evaluaran su atractivo sólo a partir de su foto en la licencia de conducir? Aunque las pruebas estandarizadas pueden aportar información útil a maestros y padres, son sólo una fotografía instántanea de lo que un niño puede hacer en un día particular.

 Parent Power by B. Power, © 1999. Portsmouth, NH: Heinemann.

Using the Library with Your Child

Your local library is a resource within your community that not only builds knowledge but also builds a lifelong love of reading. The library can become a comfortable place for you and your child to share good times together.

- **Make library time a special time.**
  Let your child get their very own library card. This gives your child a sense of importance and responsibility for their own reading education. You should also have your own library card. When you bring your child to the library, stay and enjoy the library yourself. While your child is browsing for books that interest her, spend time with her or find books for yourself. You can select books that you want to share with your child or adult books that you want to read on your own. Make library time a regular part of your schedule, preferably once a week. This gives your child something to look forward to each week.
- **Enjoy other library resources.**
  There are a variety of resources for you and your child at your local library. Libraries have thousands of wonderful books for you to borrow and enjoy. However, books are not the only materials offered to you from your library. Most libraries have a section that offers current and back issues of the most popular magazines and newspapers. In addition to reading materials, most libraries offer videos, music, and books on cassette.
- **Go to special events.**
  There are a variety of activities and programs available. Most public libraries have a special time for children called "Story Hour." At this time your child is read to by an experienced storyteller. Many times these sessions include drama and question-and-answer periods. Some other activities that may be offered at your library are puppet shows, guest speakers, movies, arts and crafts, and reading programs. Call your local library to get a schedule of upcoming events.

Usar la biblioteca con su hijo(a)

Su biblioteca local es un recurso en su comunidad que no sólo desarrolla los conocimientos, sino que también crea un amor por la lectura durante toda la vida. La biblioteca puede convertirse en un lugar confortable para usted y su hijo(a) donde pueden compartir momentos agradables juntos.

- **Haga que el tiempo dedicado a la biblioteca sea especial.**
  Deje que su hijo(a) tenga su propia tarjeta de de visitante a la biblioteca. Esto da a su hijo(a) un sentido de importancia y responsabilidad en cuanto a su propia educación en la lectura. Usted debe tener también su propia tarjeta de la biblioteca. Cuando lleve a su hijo(a) a la biblioteca, quédese un rato y disfrútela. Mientras que su hijo(a) explora en busca de libros que le interesen, dedique tiempo a estar con él o ella o busque libros para usted. Puede seleccionar libros que desea compartir con su hijo(a) o libros para adultos que usted quiere leer a solas. Haga que el tiempo dedicado a la biblioteca sea una parte habitual de su programación, preferiblemente una vez a la semana. Esto le da a su hijo la oportunidad de anticipar algo agradable todas las semanas.

- **Disfrute de otros recursos de la biblioteca.**
  Hay una variedad de recursos para usted y su hijo(a) en su biblioteca local. Las bibliotecas tienen miles de libros maravillosos para que usted los pida prestados y disfrute de ellos. No obstante, los libros no son los únicos materiales que ofrece su biblioteca. La mayoría de las mismas tienen una sección que ofrece ediciones actuales y pasadas de las revistas y periódicos más populares. Además de materiales de lectura, la mayor parte de las bibliotecas ofrecen vídeos, música y libros en cintas de audio.

- **Asista a eventos especiales.**
  Hay una diversidad de actividades y programas a su disposición. La mayoría de las bibliotecas públicas tiene un horario especial para niños llamado "Story Hour" o "La hora del cuentecito". En esa actividad una persona con experiencia en relatar cuentos lee a su hijo(a). Muchas veces esas sesiones incluyen dramas y sesiones de preguntas y respuestas. Otras actividades que se pueden ofrecer en su biblioteca son espectáculos de títeres, oradores invitados, películas, artesanías y programas de lectura. Llame a su biblioteca local para obtener una programación de los eventos futuros.

Talking with Your Child About School

"What did you do in school today?"
"Nuthin'. Can I go outside and play now?"

Though the world may have changed a lot since you went to school, it seems like this classic exchange between parents and children at the end of each day always stays the same. When children first come home, they are often tired. They may also feel a bit overwhelmed by all that has happened during the day. Talking about the day immediately with a parent may not be something they want to do. But children do need to talk about school with their families—there is so much that they are learning each day, and so many new social situations they will need help in understanding. Here are some ways to help your child talk more about school with your family:

- **You talk first.**
  Instead of asking your child, "What did you do in school today?" tell a quick story from your own day. It might be something funny, like going to a meeting first thing in the morning looking like a drowned rat because you forgot your umbrella that day. Or it might be something a little exciting, like seeing a big fire on your way to do some grocery shopping.
- **Wait.**
  Allow your child to go outside and play to run off some energy. Or let your child watch an educational video or read a book for awhile. Some children need to have some time to themselves before they are ready to talk about their day.
- **Break bread together.**
  Nothing fosters good conversation more than eating together. Turn off the television, put out some cookies or fruit after school, and sit together.
- **Ask about specific school or classroom events.**
  Pay attention to newsletters or notes that come from the school or your child's teacher for upcoming themes, field trips, or class activities. If you ask, "Who did you sit with on the field trip?" you'll have a better chance of getting your child to talk about the event.
- **Expect some days to have more talk than others.**
  Everyone has days when they are eager to talk with others, and days when they want more time alone. Children are no different. There will be days when there are many long pauses and breaks in the conversation, and other days when you laugh very hard together. Accept these differing moods as a normal part of the relationship you have with your child.

Hablar con su hijo(a) sobre la escuela

"¿Qué hiciste en la escuela hoy?"
"Nada. ¿Puedo salir y jugar ahora?"

Aunque el mundo puede haber cambiado mucho desde que usted asistió a la escuela, parece que este clásico intercambio de preguntas entre padres e hijos(as) al final de cada día siempre permanece igual. Cuando los niños acaban de llegar a la casa, se sienten cansados. También pueden sentirse un poco abrumados por todo lo que ha sucedido durante el día. Hablar sobre cómo transcurrió el día inmediatamente con uno de los padres puede ser algo que no deseen hacer. Pero los niños sí necesitan hablar sobre la escuela con sus familias. Es tanto lo que aprenden cada día, y son tantas las situaciones sociales nuevas que enfrentan, que hay que ayudarlos a comprender. Estas son algunas formas de ayudar a su hijo(a) a hablar más sobre la escuela con su familia:

- **Hable usted primero.**
  En lugar de preguntar a su hijo: "¿qué hiciste en la escuela hoy?", cuente una anécdota corta de su propio día. Puede ser algo gracioso, como que la primera cosa que hizo por la mañana fue asistir a una reunión y lucir como una rata mojada porque olvidó su sombrilla ese día. O puede tratarse de algo un poco emocionante, como ver un gran incendio en el camino al supermercado.
- **Espere.**
  Deje que su hijo(a) salga y juegue para que consuma un poco de energía. O deje que su hijo(a) vea un vídeo educativo o lea un libro durante un rato. Algunos niños necesitan tener un tiempo para sí mismos antes de estar listos para hablar sobre cómo transcurrió su día.
- **Coman algo juntos.**
  Nada favorece más una buena conversación que comer juntos. Apague el televisor, saque algunas galletitas o frutas después del regreso de la escuela, y siéntense juntos.
- **Pregunte sobre eventos específicos de la escuela o la clase.**
  Ponga atención a los boletines o notas provenientes de la escuela o del maestro de su hijo(a) sobre los próximos temas, excursiones o actividades de clase. Si usted pregunta: "¿Con quién te sentaste en la excursión?", tendrá más posibilidades de lograr que su hijo(a) hable sobre la actividad.
- **Espere tener más conversación en algunos días que en otros.**
  Todo el mundo tiene días en que desea hablar con otros, y días en que desea más tiempo a solas. Los niños no son diferentes. Existirán días en los que habrá muchas pausas largas e interrupciones en la conversación, y otros días en los que reirán juntos a carcajadas. Acepte esos diferentes estados de ánimo como un aspecto normal de la relación que mantiene con su hijo(a).

 Parent Power by B. Power, © 1999. Portsmouth, NH: Heinemann.

Reading with Your Child

There aren't many rules for good reading experiences at home. You know your child best, and as you read together, you will learn about your child's unique book preferences, favorite times for reading, and best ways for sharing the book together. The following tips will help you and your child look forward to reading together at home:

- **Don't emphasize correctness in reading the book.**
  Unless your child misreads a word or words to the point where the story can no longer be understood, don't correct them. Even skilled adult readers occasionally misread individual words without realizing it. As long as the meaning of the story is still clear, you needn't break the rhythm and flow of the text with corrections.
- **Remember that even small amounts of time reading together are worthwhile.**
  Don't worry if many days don't allow for more than ten or fifteen minutes of reading together. What matters is that you have daily reading together, so that your child sees this as a cherished routine.
- **Read books that extend the story over days and weeks.**
  Even young children can enjoy adventures in chapter books. If you do read a lengthy story, make sure you have a brief period before the day's reading when you and your child recap what has happened in the story thus far.
- **Don't be afraid to abandon a book.**
  Some of the most wonderful books ever written just don't lend themselves to oral reading, or won't suit you and your child's tastes. All good readers occasionally abandon a book.
- **Don't be afraid to reread a book.**
  Children love rhythms, routines, and repetitions. Though it may drive *you* nuts to read *Cinderella* for the fourteenth time this year, many children are turned on to reading through one book read over and over and over again.

Leer con su hijo(a)

No hay reglas rígidas para tener una buena experiencia de lectura en el hogar. Usted conoce mejor a su hijo(a), y mientras leen juntos, usted aprenderá las preferencias particulares de su hijo(a), sus horarios de lectura favoritos, y las mejores formas de compartir un libro juntos. Las sugerencias siguientes ayudarán a que usted y a su hijo(a) disfruten de la lectura en el hogar.

- **No ponga énfasis en la corrección al leer el libro.**
  A menos que su hijo(a) lea mal una palabra o palabras de tal manera que ya no se pueda entender la historia, no le haga correcciones. Aun los lectores adultos experimentados leen mal ocasionalmente palabras individuales sin darse cuenta. Mientras que el significado de la historia quede claro, usted no necesita romper el ritmo y el curso del texto con correcciones.
- **Recuerde que incluso pequeños ratos de lectura conjunta son valiosos.**
  No se preocupe si hay días en que no puede dedicar más de diez o quince minutos a leer juntos. Lo que importa es que lean juntos a diario, de forma que su hijo(a) vea que es una rutina apreciada.
- **Escoja libros con relatos que leerán a lo largo de varios días o semanas.**
  Incluso a los niños pequeños les gusta leer cuentos de aventura en libros que tienen varios capítulos. Si lee una historia larga, asegúrese de disponer de un breve tiempo antes de la lectura del día para recapitular sobre lo que ocurrió en la historia hasta ese momento.
- **No tema abandonar un libro.**
  Algunos de los libros más maravillosos que se han escrito simplemente no se prestan a una lectura oral, o no se adaptan a los gustos de usted y su hijo(a). Todos los buenos lectores abandonan ocasionalmente un libro.
- **No tema volver a leer un libro.**
  A los niños les encantan los ritmos, las rutinas y las repeticiones. Aunque a usted pueda enloquecerlo leer *Cenicienta* por decimocuarta vez este año, muchos niños se acostumbran a leer el mismo libro una y otra vez.

Meeting with Your Child's Teacher
Part 1: Preparation

Meetings with a teacher over your child's work is a time to celebrate good learning that is taking place in the classroom—as well as to make plans for how you can work together to foster even more growth. Here are some things to think about before you go to the meeting:

- **Set a convenient time for the meeting.**
  Allow yourself a few extra minutes in your schedule to relax before the meeting so that you go into the conference relaxed and focused. It helps to write down specific questions for the teacher, so that your notes can jog your memory about what you want to discuss.
- **Be punctual and limit your meeting time, especially when other parents are scheduled before and after your conference with the teacher.**
  If you find there are more issues to discuss and time is limited, schedule another meeting. This gives you more time to think about the issues, and it also allows other parents who may be waiting to have their turn.
- **If you find that there is something you do not understand about the purpose of the meeting, such as test result scores or jargon used to request a meeting, be sure to ask for an explanation.**
  Many other parents have asked the same questions. Explaining new information for parents is a responsibility most teachers love!
- **Make sure it is clear whether or not your child is expected to attend the conference.**
  Some teachers encourage students to participate with parents in the meeting. Other teachers and parents prefer that students not be present to discuss sensitive information. If the setup of the conference makes you uncomfortable, be sure to call ahead and discuss your concerns before the meeting date.

By taking a little time to think about the purpose of the conference in advance, everyone will make the most of this chance to get to know each other better and to make good plans for your child.

Reunirse con el maestro de su hijo(a), Parte 1: Preparación

Las reuniones con un maestro sobre el trabajo de su hijo son ocasiones para celebrar el buen aprendizaje que tiene lugar en la clase, al igual que para hacer planes en conjunto con el fin de fomentar un desarrollo aún mayor. Aquí presentamos algunos puntos en los que debe pensar antes de ir a la reunión:

- **Fije una hora conveniente para la reunión.**
  Tómese unos minutos adicionales en su programación para sentirse relajado antes de la reunión, de manera que acuda a la conferencia tranquilo y con la mente enfocada en lo que va a tratar. Resulta útil escribir las preguntas específicas que hará al maestro, a fin de que sus notas puedan estimular su memoria en cuanto a lo que desea tratar.
- **Sea puntual y limite el tiempo de su reunión, especialmente cuando otros padres tienen cita para ver al maestro antes y después de su conferencia.**
  Si usted considera que hay más problemas que tratar y el tiempo es limitado, pida otra cita con el maestro. Esto le da más tiempo para pensar acerca de los problemas, y da una oportunidad a otros padres que pueden estar esperando su turno.
- **Si considera que hay algo que no entiende sobre el propósito de la reunión, tal como el resultado de una prueba o una expresión usada para solicitar una reunión, asegúrese de pedir una explicación.**
  Muchos otros padres han hecho las mismas preguntas. Explicar la nueva información a los padres es una responsabilidad que les encanta a la mayoría de los maestros.
- **Asegúrese de que está claro si se espera que su hijo(a) asista o no a la conferencia.**
  Algunos maestros alientan a los estudiantes a participar en las reuniones junto con los padres. Otros maestros y padres prefieren que los estudiantes no estén presentes cuando hablan sobre asuntos que pueden herir su sensibilidad. Si la preparación de la conferencia le hace sentirse incómodo, llame primero y exprese sus preocupaciones antes de la fecha de la reunión.

Si dedica algún tiempo a pensar con anticipación sobre el propósito de la reunión, todos aprovecharán al máximo esta oportunidad de conocerse cada uno mejor y de hacer buenos planes para su hijo(a).

© 1999. Portsmouth, NH: Heinemann.

Meeting with Your Child's Teacher
Part 2: The Main Event

There are a few butterflies in the stomach, a last-minute flurry to make sure everything is in place, and some quick deep breaths to calm any jitters. This may not be your behavior before a conference with a teacher, but it certainly reflects the final moments of preparation for most teachers before a meeting with a parent. There is nervousness on both sides before parent-teacher conferences—but also lots of happy anticipation. You share a common goal and delight—fostering more learning and social growth in your child.

Most conferences take place in the classroom, and with good reason. It's easier to understand how your child fits into the class community if you're sitting in the midst of where the child works and plays with others. Before the conference begins, you might want to look around for evidence of your child's work. The teacher can tell you what projects or activities around the classroom your child naturally gravitates to. What activities does your child need more exposure to? As you discuss your child's academic work, ask to see specific assignments or projects. What projects or units is the class working on currently? Ask your teacher what games or activities at home could be used to extend classroom activities.

As the meeting is ending, you might want to set a future meeting time, or just exchange convenient times for correspondence. If you can only make calls during the day, does the teacher have a free period during the school day when he or she can receive calls? How late can you or the teacher receive calls at night? Do either of you prefer day or evening calls? Although you may not need to contact each other right away, knowing convenient times will make contact easier in the future.

Make sure that you also take a few moments to discuss the meeting with your child. Whether your child has attended the meeting or not, the goals and information discussed will be helpful to share. Children will also be reassured about the positive purposes of most parent-teacher conferences, and will learn to look forward to future meetings you have with the teacher.

Reunirse con el maestro de su hijo(a), Parte 2: La reunión en sí

Hay padres que sienten unas punzadas en el estómago y un nerviosismo de último minuto preocupándose de que todo esté en orden, y tienen que respirar profundo para calmar cualquier inquietud. Quizás usted no se comporte así antes de una conferencia con el maestro, pero sí puede ser la experiencia de la mayor parte de los maestros antes de una reunión con un padre. Hay nerviosismo en ambas partes antes de las conferencias entre padres y maestros. También hay mucha anticipación feliz. Se comparte un objetivo y un deleite común: fomentar un mayor aprendizaje y desarrollo social en su hijo(a).

La mayoría de las conferencias tienen lugar en un aula, y por un buen motivo. Resulta más fácil entender cómo se adapta su hijo(a) a la clase si usted se sienta en medio del lugar donde su hijo(a) trabaja y juega con los otros. Antes de que comience la conferencia, usted puede dar un vistazo para tener una evidencia del trabajo de su hijo(a). El maestro puede decirle cuáles son los proyectos o actividades hacia los cuales se inclina más su hijo(a). ¿En que actividades necesita su hijo(a) tener una mayor participación? Cuando hable del trabajo académico de su hijo(a), pregunte cuáles son las tareas o los proyectos específicos. ¿En qué proyectos o unidades está trabajando la clase actualmente? Pregunte al maestro qué juegos o actividades se pueden realizar en la casa para extender las actividades de la clase.

Cuando esté terminando la reunión, usted puede fijar una fecha para una reunión futura, o simplemente establecer las horas convenientes para comunicarse. Si usted sólo puede realizar llamadas durante el día, averigüe si el maestro tiene un tiempo libre durante el día escolar para recibir llamadas. Pregúntele hasta qué hora puede el maestro recibir llamadas por la noche. Y dígale hasta que hora puede recibir llamadas usted. Determinen si el uno y el otro prefieren las llamadas de día o de noche. Aunque usted no necesite ponerse en contacto con el maestro ahora mismo, el hecho de saber cuáles son las horas más apropiadas para llamarlo hará más fácil el contacto en el futuro.

Tome unos minutos para hablar sobre la reunión con su hijo(a). Ya sea que su hijo(a) haya asistido o no a la reunión, será útil compartir las metas y la información sobre las que se han hablado. Los niños se sentirán más seguros al saber el propósito positivo de la mayor parte de las conferencias de padres y maestros, y aprenderán a desear reuniones futuras que usted tenga con el maestro.

Nutrition: Raising Low-Fat Kids

It's tough to raise low-fat kids in a high-fat world, and the task gets more challenging all the time. Recent statistics show that the diets of children are higher in fat than ever, and this translates into much greater risk of heart disease and obesity at an earlier age.

Luckily, greater awareness of the issue of too much fat in children's diets has led to recent reforms. The new United States federal guidelines for school lunch programs are reducing fat in diets. But it's still hard for parents and teachers to fight the relentless advertising pitches of junk- and fast-food companies aimed at our children.

If you want to help trim the fat in your child's diet, think of small steps rather than big changes at the start. Any kid will balk if the nightly snack of a bowl of chips is replaced with a plate of carrot sticks. There are other substitutions that are less likely to bring out howls of protest. Replace a bag of chips with a bowl of air-popped popcorn or a plate of pretzels. Instead of high-fat ice cream, how about low-fat frozen yogurt? If the substitutions involve a gradual shift toward lower-fat versions of favorite snacks, kids often do not even notice a difference in taste.

Resist the urge to use food as a treat or reward—even if it's a healthy, low-fat food. Instead, reward particularly good behavior or special achievements in other ways. Staying up an extra fifteen minutes past bedtime to read a book with Dad, or playing a game of checkers with Mom is healthier than any food when it comes to your family's well-being. The more kids see food as a fuel, and the less they see it as a sign of love, the healthier their eating habits will be.

 Parent Power by B. Power, © 1999. Portsmouth, NH: Heinemann.

La Nutrición: Criar niños habituados a un bajo contenido de grasa

Es difícil criar niños habituados a un bajo contenido de grasa en un mundo consumidor de grasas, y esta tarea presenta un desafío cada vez mayor. Las estadísticas recientes revelan que las dietas de los niños tienen un contenido de grasa mayor que nunca antes, y esto se traduce en un riesgo mucho mayor de enfermedades del corazón y obesidad a una edad más temprana.

Afortunadamente, la toma de conciencia de este problema en las dietas infantiles ha conducido a recientes reformas. Las nuevas pautas federales de los Estados Unidos para los programas de almuerzos escolares están reduciendo la grasa en las dietas. Pero aún resulta difícil para padres y maestros luchar contra la despiadada campaña publicitaria de las compañías de comida de mala calidad y comida rápida dirigida a nuestros hijos(as).

Si usted desea ayudar a regular la grasa en la dieta de su hijo(a), piense en dar pequeños pasos en vez de hacer grandes cambios al principio. Cualquier niño se frustrará si la comida ligera de todas las noches consistente en un plato de papas fritas se reemplaza por uno de trocitos de zanahoria. Existen otras sustituciones que tienen menos posibilidad de provocar alaridos de protesta. Reemplace una bolsa de papas fritas por rositas de maíz o un plato de pretzels. En lugar de helados con alto contenido de grasa, ¿no sería mejor un yogurt helado bajo en grasa? Si las sustituciones implican un cambio gradual hacia versiones de sus meriendas favoritas con un menor contenido de grasa, los niños ni siquiera notarán una diferencia en el gusto.

Resista el impulso de usar comidas como un trato o recompensa, aun cuando sean saludables o con bajo contenido de grasa. En lugar de eso, recompense particularmente el buen comportamiento o los logros especiales de otras formas. Estar despierto por quince minutos más después de la hora habitual de ir a la cama para leer un libro con papá, o jugar una partida de damas con mamá es más saludable que cualquier comida y contribuye al bienestar de su familia. Mientras más niños vean la comida como un combustible y menos la vean como un signo de amor, más saludables serán su hábitos alimenticios.

by B. Power, © 1999. Portsmouth, NH: Heinemann.

The Power of a Map

Where would we be without maps? Probably where we usually end up—at the nearest gas station asking directions! Because maps are such a common sight, we can take all the learning they provide for granted. But for children, maps can be a source of almost endless fascination. Because children enjoy making and using maps, they can be used as a tool to help children develop a sense of place, learn geography, develop spatial intelligence, and learn how to represent information visually. Here are some quick and fun activities with maps that young children enjoy:

- **A Family Map**
  You can map out with your child the floor plan of your house. Using graph paper makes this especially enjoyable, and it also ties in some math activity involving geometry and proportion. You can label different places in the map as family member territories: Who uses what chair most? What path gets the most traffic?
- **Color the World**
  Buy an old world atlas at a rummage sale or used book store, and have your child color in the countries of Europe with you. As you color, compare the placement and names of the countries on the old atlas with maps from a new atlas. Children love this activity, and they quickly learn that the boundaries and names of countries change, even though the physical properties of the continents (mountains, rivers, valleys) stay the same.
- **Play Penny Place**
  Put a large map of the world, the United States or Canada, or your state on the floor. Stand back at least six feet, and use a stack of pennies to toss at different spots. You might choose towns, countries, states, or provinces. The game requires knowledge of geography and a little athletic skill.

Parent Power by B. Power, © 1999. Portsmouth, NH: Heinemann.

El poder de un mapa

¿Dónde estaríamos si no existieran mapas? Probablemente donde terminamos casi siempre:—
¡en la estación de gasolina más cercana pidiendo instrucciones! Dado que los mapas son algo tan
común, podemos dar por descontado todo el conocimiento que brindan. Pero para los niños, los
mapas pueden ser una fuente de fascinación casi inagotable. Ya que a los niños les gusta hacerlos
y usarlos, se pueden usar como herramienta para ayudar a los niños a desarrollar un sentido de
orientación, aprender geografía, desarrollar la inteligencia espacial y aprender cómo representar
la información visualmente. A continuación le presentamos algunas actividades rápidas y
entretenidas con mapas que le encantarán a su hijo(a):

- **Un mapa de la casa**
  Usted puede hacer con su hijo(a) un plano de su casa. Si esta actividad se hace con papel
  cuadriculado, resultará interesante y también implicará alguna tarea de matemáticas relacionada
  con la geometría o las proporciones. Usted puede marcar diferentes lugares en el mapa como te-
  rritorios de miembros de la familia: ¿Quién usa más una determinada silla? ¿Qué ruta tiene el
  mayor tráfico?
- **Colorear el mundo**
  Compre un viejo atlas del mundo en una venta de objetos usados o tienda de libros usados, y
  pida a su hijo(a) que coloree con usted los países de Europa. Mientras colorea, compare la ubi-
  cación y los nombres de los países en el viejo atlas con mapas de un nuevo atlas. A los niños les
  encanta esta actividad y aprenden con rapidez que las fronteras y nombres de los países cambia,
  aunque las propiedades físicas de los continentes (montañas, ríos, valles) permanezcan iguales.
- **Juegue a colocar los centavos**
  Ponga en el piso un mapa grande del mundo, de los Estados Unidos o Canadá, o de su estado.
  Colóquese por lo menos a seis pies de distancia y use un montoncito de centavos para lanzarlos
  al aire hacia diferentes puntos. Puede escoger pueblos, países, estados o provincias. El juego
  requiere conocimiento de geografía y algo de agilidad física.

Homework
Part 1: Setting the Stage

For hardworking parents, helping children with their homework can feel like just another chore at the end of a long day. Sometimes it's easy to fall into the trap of giving too much "help" when there's too little time. Alternatively, it can be tempting to say "okay" without checking your child's book bag when they say they've finished everything already.

Parents and children can spend a lot of time disagreeing about homework if some clear boundaries and expectations aren't in place. If you set the stage well for doing homework, you'll find that you and your child quickly get into a daily routine. That doesn't mean you both won't be snapping pencils in frustration at times over a really tough math problem—but you may also find time to giggle in delight over memories of when you did homework as a child. The following suggestions may make it easier for you to help your child get comfortable with doing homework as a regular part of their day:

- **Establish a regular time to do homework.**
  Solicit your child's help in setting the time: some kids like to do work right after school; some like to unwind from the day before tackling the books. The important thing is to be consistent, and to make sure that kids don't wait too long and become tired before their work is complete.
- **Find a well-lighted, low-traffic place for homework with necessary supplies—dictionary, pencils, paper—nearby.**
  Some kids do work better with music playing, although generally not with the TV on!
- **Let the teacher know if you think your child is struggling with their homework or if they seem to be zipping through it accurately with little effort or thought.**
  You may want to ask if the teacher sees the same behavior at school before you make a request for less work or more difficult work, but don't be afraid to offer your observations.
- **Resist the urge to reward your child after finishing homework.**
  It's easy to get into a rut of ever-escalating rewards for accomplishing this daily task. It is far better to compliment your child when they are particularly industrious, and let the accomplishment of doing the job well be the best reward.

La tarea, Parte 1: Preparativos

Para los padres que trabajan mucho, ayudar a sus hijos en su tarea puede parecerles simplemente como otra obligación más al final de un largo día. Muchas veces es fácil caer en la trampa de dar demasiada "ayuda" cuando hay muy poco tiempo. Por otra parte, puede resultar tentador decir "está bien" sin revisar la mochila de los libros de su hijo(a) cuando dice que ya ha terminado todo.

Los padres y los hijos(as) pueden dedicar mucho tiempo a expresar su desacuerdo sobre las tareas si no se sitúan algunos límites y expectativas claras. Si prepara bien las condiciones para hacer la tarea, descubrirá que usted y su hijo(a) caerán rápidamente en una rutina diaria. Esto no quiere decir que ambos no se sientan frustrados y rompan lápices en algún momento cuando se les presente un problema de matemáticas bien difícil. También puede encontrar tiempo para reírse al deleitarse con recuerdos de cuando usted hacía la tarea siendo niño. Las siguientes sugerencias pueden ayudarlo a hacer que su hijo(a) se sienta cómodo al hacer la tarea como parte habitual de su día:

- **Establezca un horario habitual para hacer la tarea.**
  Solicite la cooperación de su hijo(a) para establecer el horario: a algunos niños les gusta hacer la tarea inmediatamente después de que llegan de la escuela, a otros les gusta librarse un poco de la fatiga del día antes de dedicarse a los libros. El asunto importante es ser consecuente y asegurarse de que los niños no esperen mucho y se cansen antes de terminar su tarea.
- **Busque un lugar cerca, bien iluminado y tranquilo, donde hacer la tarea con los medios necesarios, tales como diccionarios y papel.**
  Algunos niños hacen mejor la tarea oyendo música, aunque generalmente no es así con el televisor encendido.
- **Deje saber al maestro si piensa que su hijo(a) pasa mucho trabajo con su tarea o si parece que la puede hacer correctamente con poco esfuerzo o sin pensar mucho.**
  Puede preguntarle al maestro si su hijo(a) se comporta de la misma manera después que usted haya pedido que le reduzcan la tarea o que que le den tareas más complejas, pero no tema hacer sus observaciones.
- **Resista el impulso de recompensar a su hijo después de terminar la tarea.**
  Es fácil caer en la rutina de recompensas cada vez mayores por el cumplimiento de esta tarea diaria. Es mucho mejor felicitar a su hijo(a) cuando es particularmente aplicado y deje que la mejor recompensa sea el hecho de hacer bien el trabajo.

 Parent Power by B. Power, © 1999. Portsmouth, NH: Heinemann.

Homework
Part 2: Coaching Your Child

Those who coach children all the time—the swim instructor who fine-tunes the butterfly stroke for an athlete, the musician who helps a youngster work toward better tonal quality on a clarinet—know how hard it is to balance giving good guidance with letting children practice and learn on their own. As your child's homework "coach," you are also learning that delicate balance between guiding and letting go. Here are some tips for helping you develop good teaching strategies for working with your child as they complete homework assignments:

- **Read over directions with your child, and ask them to explain the directions to you in their own words.**
  It can be very frustrating to work on an assignment for a long time, only to realize you were doing it wrong. Help your child to get started on the right track.
- **Put your child in charge of the pencil.**
  Resist the urge to write down an answer or make notes yourself.
- **If the assignment is manageable, allow your child some time alone to work on math problems or a piece of writing.**
  If you check on them every now and then, you will be able to judge whether to step in and prevent frustration. If you hover too closely while they attempt some tasks on their own, they may become nervous or dependent.
- **Ask your child to explain their reasoning for the answers they write down.**
  Since homework is meant to reinforce concepts and give kids practice with new skills, it's not enough simply to memorize a procedure. They need to understand it, too—and explaining it to you is a good way to help them determine what they know.
- **Break challenging tasks into smaller, more manageable pieces.**
  Model what your child needs to do if they are confused, and provide lots of praise as they take over more of the responsibility from you.

As you use these techniques consistently, you will find that your child quickly begins to anticipate when it is appropriate to ask for help—and when you will expect more independent effort. This will make homework time an easier time for all.

   Parent Power by B. Power, © 1999. Portsmouth, NH: Heinemann.

La tarea, Parte 2: Entrenar a su hijo

Aquellos que entrenan a los niños todo el tiempo —el instructor de natación que busca la perfección en la brazada de mariposa de un atleta, el músico que ayuda al joven a esforzarse por obtener una mejor calidad de tono en el clarinete— conocen lo difícil que resulta lograr el equilibrio entre guiar bien y dejar que el niño practique y aprenda por sí mismo. Como "entrenador" de la tarea de su hijo(a), usted está también aprendiendo ese delicado equilibrio entre guiar y dejar hacer. Estas son algunas sugerencias que lo ayudarán a desarrollar buenas estrategias de enseñanza mientras ayuda a su hijo(a) con las tareas.

- **Lea bien las instrucciones con su hijo(a), y pídale que le explique las mismas con sus propias palabras.**
  Puede causar mucha frustración trabajar en una tarea por mucho tiempo, sólo para darse cuenta de que la estaba haciendo mal. Ayude a su hijo(a) a comenzar el trabajo por el buen camino.
- **Ponga a su hijo(a) a cargo del lápiz.**
  Resista el impulso de escribir una respuesta o hacer notas usted mismo.
- **Si la tarea es algo que su hijo(a) puede manejar por su cuenta, concédale un tiempo para que trabaje en los problemas de matemáticas o en tareas de redacción.**
  Si le da una vuelta cada cierto tiempo, usted podrá juzgar si debe intervenir y prevenir la frustración. Si ronda muy cerca mientras su hijo(a) intenta realizar algunas tareas por sí mismo, se puede poner nervioso o hacerse dependiente.
- **Pida a su hijo que explique su razonamiento para las respuestas que escribe.**
  Ya que la tarea está concebida para reforzar los conceptos y darle práctica a los niños en las nuevas habilidades, no es suficiente memorizar simplemente un procedimiento. Es necesario que su hijo(a) lo entienda también, y explicárselo a usted es una buena forma de ayudarlo a determinar lo que sabe.
- **Divida las tareas difíciles en partes más pequeñas, más manejables.**
  Planee lo que su hijo(a) necesita hacer si se confunde, y hágale muchos elogios cuando asume mayor responsabilidad.

Cuando emplee estas técnicas en forma consecuente, se dará cuenta de que su hijo(a) comienza rápidamente a saber por anticipado cuándo es adecuado pedir ayuda, y cuándo usted espera más esfuerzos independientes. Esto hará que el tiempo dedicado a las tareas resulte más fácil para todos.

 Parent Power by B. Power, © 1999. Portsmouth, NH: Heinemann.

Everyday Math

So what does a bologna sandwich in a lunch box have to do with learning math? Everything—in classrooms where everyday experiences with math problems are valued. Your child might be asked to survey classmates to discover what they have packed in their lunch boxes, and then to chart the results on a graph. Comparing the number of bologna sandwiches to peanut butter sandwiches to hot lunch purchases leads children into concepts of numbers, percentages, and visually representing information.

Children still learn the math facts and concepts that were valued when you were a student—but they are often learning them in different ways. Here are some newer practices in math that are used to help children see math as a natural, everyday process.

- **Open-Ended Problems**
  Children are being given more math problems that don't have a clear "right" answer. No one knows how many children prefer cats to dogs as pets when that survey question is asked and charted, or what the ratio is of the size of a child's hand to the length of a desktop before it is measured.
- **Hands-on, Minds-on Activities**
  You'll notice that your child is doing many more math activities beyond practicing adding, subtracting, or fractions on worksheets. Students are being pushed to find more than one route to get to an answer. What this promotes in children is a willingness to try more than once in tackling a problem, building their ability to see more complex problems later in more sophisticated ways.
- **Math Journals/Learning Logs**
  As children try out many possible solutions, they are challenged to write about their process in math so they can become more aware of the steps they take to get to an answer.

As your child develops mathematical skills, teachers and parents can work together to ensure that math is more than getting the right answer (though in the end that's important too!). Becoming a strong mathematician involves seeing more and more possibilities for using numbers to solve complicated problems, and using numbers as a tool to understand the world. Encourage your child to play with math, and notice the math in tasks you do every day.

Las matemáticas de cada día

¿Qué tiene que ver un sándwich de bologna en una cajita de almuerzo con aprender matemáticas? Pues tiene mucho que ver con una clase donde las experiencias diarias con los problemas de matemáticas se valoran. A su hijo(a) se le puede pedir que realice una encuesta a sus compañeros para conocer lo que han puesto en sus cajita de almuerzo y representar luego el resultado en un gráfico. Comparar el número de sándwiches de bologna con el de sándwiches de mantequilla de maní y con las compras de comida caliente lleva a los niños a comprender mejor los conceptos numéricos, los porcentajes y la representación visual de la información.

Hoy en día, los niños aprenden los mismos conceptos matemáticos que se valoraban cuando usted era estudiante, pero por lo general hoy se aprenden de otra manera. A continuación presentamos algunas prácticas nuevas que se usan para ayudar a los niños a ver las matemáticas como un proceso natural y cotidiano.

- **Problemas sin respuesta exacta.**
  A los niños se les están dando más problemas de matemáticas que no tienen la misma respuesta exacta en toda situación. Nadie conoce cuántos niños prefieren gatos a perros como mascotas cuando se hace esa pregunta en una encuesta y se representa en una tabla, o cuál es la relación entre el tamaño de la mano de un niño y la longitud de la parte superior del escritorio antes de tomar las medidas.
- **Actividades de práctica directa.**
  Usted observará que su hijo(a) está haciendo muchas más actividades de matemáticas más allá de la práctica de suma y resta, o de fracciones en hojas de trabajo. A los estudiantes se les enseña a encontrar más de una ruta para llegar a una respuesta. Lo que esto promueve en los niños es una voluntad de intentar más de una vez cómo abordar un problema, y desarrolla su habilidad de enfocar otros problemas más complejos en el futuro.
- **Diarios de matemáticas/cuadernos de aprendizaje.**
  Mientras los niños investigan soluciones posibles, se les presenta la oportunidad de escribir sobre el proceso en matemáticas de manera que puedan ganar en conocimiento sobre los pasos que dan para llegar a una respuesta.

Mientras su hijo(a) desarrolla habilidades matemáticas, los maestros y padres pueden actuar en conjunto para cerciorarse de que las matemáticas sean más que una cuestión de dar la respuesta correcta (aunque, en última instancia, esto es importante también) Llegar a ser un buen matemático implica ver más y más posibilidades de usar números para resolver problemas complicados y usarlos como medios para entender el mundo. Anime a su hijo(a) a jugar con las matemáticas y observe que las matemáticas diarias son tareas que usted realiza cada día.

 Parent Power by B. Power, © 1999. Portsmouth, NH: Heinemann.

Math at Home

Many parents rarely use the words *fun* and *math* in the same sentence, especially on nights when it's time to balance the checkbook! But there are simple games you can play with your child as you're going about normal, daily tasks that can build their math abilities. And in the process, you'll have fun together as you complete household chores.

- **Pizza Math**
  Have your child divvy up a pizza with you, and you can talk about what percentage each piece is of the pie. This activity can help your child learn fractions and percentages.
- **Guessing Games**
  Before you begin folding a load of clothes, have your child take a guess about how many items of clothing there are in the dryer. You can play the same game with guessing how many things are in the dishwasher. This game helps children gain a sense of volume and quantity.
- **Sorting Games**
  When you're cleaning out a cupboard or closet, have your child sort items into types—boxes of cereal; numbers of cans of fruit versus number of cans of soup. You can extend this game by having the child calculate the percentage of one item to the whole if your child is studying fractions at school.
- **Graphing**
  Point out interesting graphs in magazines, newspapers, and on cereal boxes. By helping your child learn to read the margins of graphs, you'll build their awareness of how mathematical findings can be presented visually.
- **The Shape Game**
  At the dinner table or in the car, play a game to see how many items of one shape (or how many different shapes) can be found within a time limit. Rectangles or circles will give the highest number of items; try for offbeat shapes such as ovals to push your child to see a range of shapes in the world around them.

Once you begin to notice shapes, numbers, and graphs around you, your family will quickly develop their own favorite math games. And who knows—if you have a child who loves math, you may eventually have a teenager who likes helping you balance that checkbook!

Las matemáticas en el hogar

Muchos padres usan muy poco las palabras *diversión* y *matemáticas* en la misma oración, especialmente la noche cuando es el momento de hallar el saldo en la cuenta de cheques. Pero existen juegos simples que puede practicar con su hijo(a) mientras usted realiza actividades cotidianas que pueden servir para desarrollar sus habilidades en matemáticas. Y sobre la marcha, la pasarán bien juntos mientras usted realiza los quehaceres domésticos.

- **Matemáticas con pizzas.**
  Pida a su hijo(a) que divida una pizza junto con usted y aproveche para hablar sobre qué porcentaje de la pizza completa es cada porción. Esta actividad puede ayudar a su hijo a aprender las fracciones y los porcentajes.
- **Juegos de adivinar.**
  Antes de que empiece a doblar un bulto de ropa, pida a su hijo(a) que adivine cuántas piezas de ropa hay en la secadora. Usted puede hacer el mismo juego adivinado cuántas cosas hay en la lavadora de platos. Este juego ayuda a los niños a obtener un sentido de volumen y cantidad.
- **Juegos de clasificación.**
  Cuando esté limpiando un armario o clóset, pida a su hijo(a) que clasifique los objetos en tipos, por ejemplo: cajas de cereal, número de latas de fruta con respecto al número de latas de sopa. Usted puede extender este juego haciendo que el niño calcule el porcentaje de un objeto con respecto al total si su hijo(a) está estudiando fracciones en la escuela.
- **Gráficas.**
  Señale gráficas interesantes en revistas, periódicos y en cajas de cereales. Al ayudar a su hijo(a) a aprender a leer la información a lo largo del margen de las gráficas, usted le desarrollará el conocimiento de cómo los resultados matemáticos se pueden presentar visualmente.
- **El juego de las formas.**
  En la mesa del comedor o en el carro, haga un juego para ver cuántos objetos de una forma determinada (o cuántas formas diferentes) se pueden hallar en un período de tiempo limitado. Los rectángulos o círculos darán el mayor número de objetos; busque figuras originales tales como óvalos para incitar a su hijo(a) a observar una amplia gama de formas en el mundo que lo rodea.

Una vez que comience a observar formas, números y gráficos alrededor de usted, su familia desarrollará con rapidez sus propios juegos matemáticos favoritos. Y quién sabe, si a su niño(a) le gustan las matemáticas, con el tiempo tendrá un adolescente que lo podrá ayudar a hallar el saldo en la libreta de cheques.

 Parent Power by B. Power, © 1999. Portsmouth, NH: Heinemann.

Displaying and Storing Children's Work

There isn't a refrigerator large enough in the world to display the drawings a youngster creates in an average month. As the number of science projects, awards, sketches, and notes mounts throughout the early years of school, parents face the dilemma of deciding what to save and display and what to throw out.

Our own moms saved those lumpy clay vases from Mother's Day (never mind that they couldn't hold water). These days, children bring home more work than ever, and there are more than a few items to cherish. Here are some simple tips for organizing, sorting, and sharing your child's work:

- **Pick a time each week or month to sort through what's been brought home, selecting only an item or two to save.**
  You might do this on the night when you have a regular chore, such as paying the bills or doing the laundry, as a way to jog your memory.
- **Let your child have a voice in selections.**
  You may think that a choice is strange, but often there is a story behind why a particular drawing or project is special to your child. Write this information about the selection as a brief caption to the work.
- **Save work in three-ring binders or photo albums.**
  It's easier to keep track of work and pare down choices if you limit work from a year or two to fitting in an album.
- **Photograph larger work.**
  Massive science projects or pieces of art can be photographed and captioned if they are too large to be saved.
- **Share the wealth.**
  There are creative ways to recycle work that isn't being saved. Simple sketches and finger paintings make great wrapping paper, or can be turned into greeting cards for friends and family. A dozen sketches can be recycled as a calendar. You can even laminate larger pictures to make placemats to give as gifts.

It takes time to organize and save your child's best work. But years from now that box of school and home treasures will be one of the most cherished items in the attic.

 Parent Power by B. Power, © 1999. Portsmouth, NH: Heinemann.

Exhibir y guardar el trabajo de los niños

No existe un refrigerador lo suficientemente grande en el mundo para exhibir los dibujos que un niño crea en un mes promedio. En la medida en que el número de proyectos, premios, dibujos y notas aumenta a través de los primeros años escolares, los padres enfrentan el dilema de decidir qué deben conservar y exhibir y qué deben desechar.

Nuestras propias madres conservaban regalos inservibles, como floreros de barro del Día de las Madres. Hoy en día los niños traen a casa más trabajos que nunca, y hay más de un objeto para apreciar. Aquí damos algunas sugerencias para organizar, clasificar y compartir el trabajo de su hijo(a):

- **Escoja un rato una vez a la semana o al mes para clasificar lo que se ha llevado a casa, seleccionando sólo un objeto o dos para conservar.**
  Usted puede hacer esto la noche en la que tiene una tarea doméstica habitual, tal como pagar las cuentas o lavar, como una forma de estimular su memoria.
- **Deje que su hijo(a) opine en las selecciones.**
  A usted le puede resultar extraña alguna preferencia de su hijo(a), pero a veces hay una historia detrás de por qué un dibujo o proyecto particular es especial para su hijo(a). Anote esta información acerca de la selección a manera de breve subtítulo del trabajo.
- **Conserve el trabajo en carpetas de tres argollas o álbumes de fotos.**
  Es más fácil seguir la evolución del trabajo escolar y reducir el número de muestras que usted guarde, si limita las muestras de un año o dos a las que quepan en un álbum.
- **Tome fotos de los trabajos más grandes.**
  Cuando los trabajos de ciencias o de arte resultan demasiado grandes, es mejor fotografiarlos y guardar las fotos con una nota que los identifique.
- **Comparta la abundancia.**
  Hay muchas maneras originales de aprovechar el trabajo escolar que usted no vaya a guardar. Los dibujos y las pinturas dactilares se pueden usar para envolver regalos, o se pueden convertir en tarjetas de felicitación para amigos y familiares. Una docena de ellos puede servir para hacer un calendario. Usted puede inclusive laminar en plástico los dibujos más grandes de manera que puedan servir de manteles individuales para su propio uso o para regalar.

Toma tiempo organizar y conservar los mejores trabajos de su hijo(a). Pero dentro de unos años ese baúl de tesoros de la casa y la escuela será uno de los objetos más preciados en el ático.

 Parent Power by B. Power, © 1999. Portsmouth, NH: Heinemann.

We Know What You Want…

When it comes to surveys of what parents want from teachers, there is surprising consistency. Whether a child is entering kindergarten or is ready to graduate from high school, parents seem to have the same core beliefs about what is essential for successful relationships between parents, teachers, and students. If you could talk to us and write the rules for our classrooms, we think this is what you'd say to your children's teachers:

- **Be fair.**
  Be consistent, don't play favorites, and set up discipline procedures that are respectful. Acknowledge good deeds as well as misdeeds.
- **Communicate with us.**
  Let us know when things are going well, and tell us when they aren't going well before problems are at a crisis point.
- **Know my child.**
  Take the time to figure out each child's interests, needs, quirks, and individual talents. Children learn best when teachers know them personally and can tailor the learning to their distinct personalities.
- **Expect the best, and require it.**
  Teach each child good work habits, and push them to make their very best effort. Don't allow sloppy or half-hearted work to slip through.
- **Make homework matter.**
  Don't assign tasks that are rote, tiresome, or mindless. Let us know how to help with homework.
- **Care about my child.**
  Laugh with my child, believe in my child, and be concerned about my child when things aren't going well. If you care about my child, my child will care about what can be learned from you.

These principles are simple—but that doesn't make them easy to follow day by day. Because we do know what you want, we're trying! Let us know what other principles for teaching your child are most important to you personally. The more we communicate about what we value in schools, the better we will be able to teach your child together.

Parent Power by B. Power, © 1999. Portsmouth, NH: Heinemann.

Sabemos lo que usted desea...

Hay una coherencia sorprendente en las encuestas que se han realizado para saber qué es lo que los padres esperan de los maestros. Ya sea que el niño esté empezando el kindergarten o a punto de graduarse de la enseñanza media, los padres parecen tener las mismas creencias básicas sobre lo que es esencial para que existan relaciones exitosas entre padres, maestros y estudiantes. Si usted pudiera hablar con nosotros y escribir las reglas para nuestras clases, pensamos que esto es lo que diría a los maestros de su hijo(a):

- **Sea justo.**
  Sea consecuente, no tenga favoritismos y establezca procedimientos disciplinarios que sean respetuosos. Reconozca los actos buenos al igual que los malos.
- **Comuníquese con nosotros.**
  Déjenos saber cuando las cosas marchan bien y díganos cuando no marchan bien antes de que los problemas lleguen a un punto de crisis.
- **Conozca a mi hijo(a).**
  Tómese el tiempo de entender los intereses, necesidades, peculiaridades y talentos individuales de cada niño(a). Los niños aprenden mejor cuando los maestros los conocen personalmente y pueden adaptar el aprendizaje a sus diferentes personalidades.
- **Espere lo mejor y exíjalo.**
  Enseñe a cada niño los hábitos del buen trabajo y estimúlelo a hacer su mejor esfuerzo. No permita que se introduzca un trabajo descuidado o indiferente.
- **Haga que la tarea tenga importancia.**
  No asigne tareas que sean rutinarias, aburridas o sin sentido. Déjenos saber cómo podemos ayudar con la tarea.
- **Preocúpese por mi hijo(a).**
  Ría con mi hijo(a), confíe en mi hijo(a), y preocúpese de mi hijo(a) cuando las cosas no estén marchando bien. Si usted muestra interés en mi hijo(a), él o ella mostrará interés en lo que puede aprender de usted.

Esos principios son simples, pero no son fáciles de seguir día tras día. Ya que si sabemos lo que usted espera de nosotros, los maestros, estamos haciendo todo esfuerzo posible por cumplir. Déjenos saber cuáles son los principios de enseñanza que usted considera más importantes para su hijo(a). Mientras más nos comuniquemos acerca de lo que valoramos en las escuelas, en mejores condiciones estaremos de enseñar a su hijo(a) juntos.

 Parent Power by B. Power, © 1999. Portsmouth, NH: Heinemann.

Daily To-Do List

Everyone is busy, and it's hard to know in the midst of that busyness what is most important to get done, and what tasks we can ignore or skip. This is especially true for parents when their children begin to go to school. All parents want their children to succeed. But with the rush of work, home, and school responsibilities, it's sometimes difficult to remember the most important daily tasks for school success. Research has tracked successful students over many years, in diverse home situations. There are a few things you can do daily with your child that almost guarantee that your child will be successful in school. Completing the entire list takes less than thirty minutes a day—and it's the best half hour you could possibly spend in helping your child learn and grow.

- **Read to your child—at least ten or fifteen minutes a day.**
  Nothing matters more for future academic achievement.
- **Review homework or school assignments.**
  Know what's going on in school, and teach your child that you expect to talk about school every day together, for at least a few minutes. When problems emerge, you'll have a solid ground of communicating in place.
- **Tell family stories.**
  These stories give your child a sense of history and their place in the family. Plus, children love hearing how their parents flubbed up as kids—and survived to tell the tale as an adult!
- **Set limits for television.**
  Show your child that television is only one of many options for entertainment, learning, and relaxation.
- **Know your child's teacher.**
  Stay in touch, and let the teacher know what is and isn't working for your child in school.
- **Talk about the daily news.**
  Whether it's from the front page of the daily newspaper, or the first few minutes of the morning or evening news, help your child see their place in the larger world.

If you complete these tasks daily, you'll help your child achieve in every subject area in school. Even more important, you'll see over time how comforting these routines of talking, learning, and working together can be on even the most hectic days.

   Parent Power by B. Power, © 1999. Portsmouth, NH: Heinemann.

Lista diaria de cosas que hacer

Todo el mundo está ocupado y es difícil conocer en medio de tantas ocupaciones qué es lo más importante que se debe hacer y qué tareas podemos ignorar o pasar por alto. Esto es particularmente cierto en el caso de los padres cuando sus hijos empiezan a ir a la escuela. Todos los padres quieren que sus hijos triunfen. Pero con la presión del trabajo, la casa y las responsabilidades de la escuela, a veces es difícil recordar las tareas diarias más importantes para el éxito en la escuela. Hay investigaciones que han seguido el rastro de estudiantes exitosos durante muchos años, en diferentes situaciones en el hogar. Hay algunas cosas que puede hacer diariamente con su hijo(a) que casi garantizan que su hijo(a) tenga éxito en la escuela. Hacer la lista completa toma menos de treinta minutos al día, quizás la mejor media hora que usted puede pasar ayudando a su hijo(a) a aprender y crecer.

- **Lea a su hijo, al menos diez o quince minutos al día.**
  Nada es más importante para futuros logros académicos.
- **Revise la tarea o los deberes escolares.**
  Conozca lo que sucede en la escuela y acostumbre a su hijo(a) a hablar con usted de la escuela todos los días, al menos durante quince minutos. Cuando surjan los problemas, habrá sentado una sólida base de comunicación.
- **Cuente historias de la familia.**
  Esas historias le dan a su hijo(a) un sentido del pasado familiar y de su lugar en la familia. Además, a los niños les encanta oír cómo sus padres cometían errores de niños, y que pueden hacer esos cuentos ahora que son adultos.
- **Fije límites para la televisión.**
  Indique a su hijo(a) que la televisión es sólo una de muchas opciones para entretenerse, aprender y relajarse.
- **Conozca al maestro de su hijo(a).**
  Manténgase en contacto y deje que el maestro sepa lo que le está dando resultado a su hijo(a) en la escuela y lo que no le está dando resultado.
- **Comenten las noticias del día.**
  Ayude a su hijo(a) a entender el lugar que ocupa en el mundo comentando la primera plana del periódico o los primeros minutos del noticiero de la mañana o de la noche.

Si usted realiza estas tareas todos los días, ayudará a su hijo(a) a lograr éxito en cada asignatura en la escuela. Y aún más importante, observará a través del tiempo lo útiles que pueden ser esas rutinas de hablar, aprender y trabajar juntos, aun en los días más caóticos.

 Parent Power by B. Power, © 1999. Portsmouth, NH: Heinemann.

Praise and Self-Esteem

Plants need water to grow. Children need praise to thrive. There has been a lot written recently in the media about promoting self-esteem in children. Some "experts" say that praising kids continually is essential for promoting healthy self-esteem in children; others argue that too much praise leads to sloppy work habits and inflated egos. All this contradictory advice can leave parents a little confused when it comes to knowing the best ways and times to compliment children.

The truth is, virtually all child development research shows that the right kind of praise is essential for healthy social and emotional growth in children. The right kind of praise:

- **Compliments real achievement.**
  "Good job" or "great work" remarks from teachers or parents on mediocre work make everyone value real achievement less.
- **Comments on specific behavior.**
  Adults need to focus on exactly what was done well, with words like "I noticed you took a lot of extra time cleaning your room today, and you even lined up all your books on the shelf." Comments like these help children learn to monitor and assess their own behavior.
- **Looks for patterns of good work, rather than isolated incidents.**
  For a child who is notoriously pokey about getting chores done, setting the table without being asked one night might be noticeable—setting it three nights in a row definitely deserves some praise.
- **Nudges children to learn from their mistakes.**
  Coaching a child through homework errors, rather than just commenting on the final answers, helps a child develop confidence in their ability to learn from mistakes.

Parents know the value of complimenting and praising their children's achievements—and the more focused these words of support are, the more they will help your child. By seeing what you choose to praise, your child will gain a sense of why working hard and overcoming obstacles is so important for growth.

   Parent Power by B. Power, © 1999. Portsmouth, NH: Heinemann.

Elogios y autoestima

Igual que las plantas necesitan agua para crecer, los niños necesitan elogios para prosperar. Se ha escrito mucho recientemente en los medios de comunicación sobre la importancia de alentar la autoestima en los niños. Algunos "expertos" afirman que elogiar a los niños continuamente es esencial para promover una autoestima saludable en los niños; otros argumentan que demasiado elogio lleva a formar hábitos de trabajo pobres y egos exagerados. Todos estos consejos contradictorios pueden dejar a los padres un poco confundidos cuando tratan de informarse acerca de la mejor manera de elogiar a los niños.

La verdad es que prácticamente todas las investigaciones sobre el desarrollo infantil revelan que el elogio correcto es esencial para un desarrollo social y emocional saludable en los niños. El elogio correcto:

- **Felicita el logro real.**
  Las observaciones tales como "qué bien te quedó" o "lo hiciste muy bien" hechas por maestros o padres cuando se trata de trabajos mediocres hacen que todos valoren menos los logros reales.
- **Comenta sobre un comportamiento específico.**
  Los adultos necesitan concentrarse exactamente en lo que se ha hecho bien, con palabras tales como "He observado que dedicaste mucho tiempo a limpiar tu habitación hoy y hasta arreglaste todos tus libros en el estante." Comentarios como ése ayudan a los niños a aprender a reconocer su propio comportamiento y evaluarlo.
- **Busca patrones de buen trabajo, más bien que incidentes aislados.**
  Para un niño que es marcadamente escurridizo a la hora de realizar los quehaceres domésticos, el hecho de poner la mesa una noche, sin que se le haya pedido, puede ser notable. Pero ponerla tres noches seguidas merece definitivamente un elogio.
- **Alienta a los niños a que aprendan de sus errores.**
  Enseñar a un niño a que aprendan de sus propios errores en la tarea, en lugar de hacer un simple comentario sobre las respuestas finales, ayuda al niño a desarrollar confianza en su capacidad para aprender de sus propios errores.

Los padres conocen el valor de felicitar y elogiar a los hijos por sus logros Mientras más enfocadas estén estas palabras de apoyo, más ayudarán a su hijo(a). Al recapacitar sobre lo que usted escoge para elogiar, su hijo(a) se dará cuenta de lo importante que es para su propio desarrollo el trabajar duro y vencer los obstáculos.

Best Web Sites for Parents

We want kids and parents to be *wired* in the best possible sense of the word—to know how to use the World Wide Web as a resource to build family ties. In the past few years, many Web sites have been developed to answer parents' questions about kids and learning. There are scores of Web sites devoted to activities for promoting learning and achievement in kids, too.

If you're curious about the World Wide Web, call your local library and find out if Internet access is available for local residents. Most libraries do provide free connections, and many take reservations. Bring the following Internet addresses, and prepare to be amazed at all the resources available free for parents.

The two parent sites we recommend have won numerous national and international awards. Parent Soup and The Family Education Network are two of the largest professionally run sites for parents. Parent Soup focuses mostly on general parenting issues; The Family Education Network has a wealth of resources for building academic growth in home environments. The writing at both of these sites is lively, and the advice is practical and down-to-earth.

Family Education Network: www.familyeducation.com
Parent Soup: www.parentsoup.com

These sites will also connect you with other parent-related Web sites, as well as thoughtful and fun sites for children that the whole family can enjoy. When using the Web together, have your children do as much of the pointing and clicking as possible. As they instruct you about how they use the Internet, you will get a glimpse of how teaching and learning is changing as Internet access becomes more readily available to teachers and students.

Los mejores sitios en la Internet para los padres

Queremos que los niños y los padres estén *conectados* en el mejor sentido de la palabra, para conocer cómo se usa la World Wide Web (Red a Nivel Mundial) como recurso para crear lazos familiares. En los últimos años, se han desarrollado muchos sitios en la Red para responder a las preguntas de los padres acerca de los niños y el aprendizaje. También hay gran cantidad de sitios en la Red dedicados a actividades para promover el aprendizaje y los logros en niños.

Si siente curiosidad por la Red, llame a su bibiloteca local y averigüe si el acceso a Internet está disponible para los residentes locales. La mayoría de las bibliotecas brindan conexiones gratis y muchas aceptan reservaciones. Traiga las siguientes direcciones de Internet y prepárese para sorprenderse de todos los recursos disponibles gratis para los padres.

Los dos sitios para padres que recomendamos han ganado numerosos premios nacionales e internacionales. "Parent Soup" ("Sopa de Padres") y "The Family Education Network" ("Red de Educación Familiar") son dos de los mayores sitios dirigidos profesionalmente a los padres. "Parent Soup" enfoca fundamentalmente problemas generales de los padres; "The Family Education Network" cuenta con una abundancia de recursos para fomentar el crecimiento académico en los medios del hogar. Escribir a ambos sitios resulta animado y los consejos brindados son prácticos y realistas.

Family Education Network: www.familyeducation.com
Parent Soup: www.parentsoup.com

Estos sitios también lo conectarán con otros sitios de la Red relacionados con los padres, al igual que con sitios interesantes y divertidos para los niños de los cuales puede disfrutar toda la familia. Cuando usen la Red juntos, haga que sus hijos(as) señalen y accionen el "ratón" lo más posible. A la vez que se instruye acerca de cómo usar la Internet, usted obtendrá una visión de cómo el aprendizaje y la enseñanza están cambiando en la medida en que el acceso a Internet se hace más fácilmente disponible a maestros y estudiantes.

Portsmouth, NH: Heinemann.   *Parent Power* by B. Power, © 1999.

Meeting with a Specialist

Most children at some point in their school career will meet with a specialist. When a parent is notified that their child will need some specialized evaluation or support, they understandably can be concerned. It helps to know that it is normal for most to need this additional assistance occasionally. Usually this support is short-term, focused on a specific concern.

The issue might be a child's struggle with reading at grade level, or sudden moodiness, or struggles to get along with peers. Guidance counselors, speech pathologists, and reading specialists are all available to help your child if a need arises. Working with a specialist as soon as a need is seen often enables problems to be resolved very quickly. If you are asked to attend a meeting with a specialist, the following tips can help you make the most of this time:

- **If vocabulary or words are used that you don't understand, ask.**
  Don't let language get in the way of understanding your children and their needs.
- **Be open to recommendations.**
  Specialists have worked with many children with similar needs, and they bring a wealth of experience to the problem.
- **Find out what's next in the process.**
  Make sure you know when or if it will be determined that your child needs additional assistance.
- **Follow up in a few days or weeks with a phone call or note to the specialist, to see what is being done to assist your child.**
  The specialist should be able to report progress or changes in the plan of assistance if it is not effective.

Our school community wants every child to succeed. But even more important, we want every child and family to feel secure in knowing that our whole staff is committed to helping all students, whatever their needs. The specialists on our staff will work hard with you to make sure we are all working together to meet your child's needs.

Reunirse con un especialista

La mayoría de los niños se reunirá con un especialista en algún momento de sus cursos escolares. Cuando se le notifica a un padre que su hijo(a) necesitará algún tipo de evaluación o apoyo especializado, es comprensible que se pueda preocupar, pero ayuda a los padres el hecho de conocer que es algo normal, que la mayoría necesita esa asistencia adicional ocasionalmente. Usualmente este apoyo es por un corto plazo y se concentra en un problema específico.

El problema puede consistir en las dificultades de un niño para al nivel que se espera en su grado escolar, o un repentino mal humor, o dificultades para llevarse bien con los compañeros. Hay consejeros escolares, especialistas en dicción y especialistas de lectura que están todos a su disposición para ayudar a su hijo(a) si surge alguna necesidad. Trabajar con un especialista tan pronto se observa una necesidad permite que los problemas se resuelvan muy rápidamente. Si se le pide que asista a una reunión con un especialista, las siguientes sugerencias lo pueden ayudar a aprovechar al máximo este tiempo:

- **Si usted escucha palabras o un vocabulario que no entiende, pregunte.**
  No deje que el lenguaje obstruya la comprensión de su hijo(a) y de sus necesidades.
- **Esté abierto a las recomendaciones.**
  Los especialistas han trabajado con muchos niños con necesidades similares y tienen mucha experiencia con estos problemas.
- **Averigüe cuál es el próximo paso del proceso.**
  Cerciórese de que lo mantengan informado si su hijo(a) necesita ayuda adicional y cuándo la recibiría.
- **Dé seguimiento mediante una llamada telefónica o nota al especialista dentro de unos días o semanas, para ver lo que se ha hecho para ayudar a su hijo(a).**
  El especialista debe estar en condiciones de informar el progreso logrado o los cambios en el plan de ayuda si éste no resulta eficaz.

Nuestro deseo en la escuela es que su hijo(a) triunfe. Pero lo que es más importante, queremos que cada niño y cada familia se sientan seguros al conocer que todo nuestro personal está comprometido a ayudar a todos los estudiantes, cualesquiera que sean sus necesidades. Los especialistas de nuestro personal trabajarán arduamente con usted para asegurar que todos nuestros esfuerzos estén coordinados con el fin de satisfacer las necesidad de sus hijo(a).

  Parent Power by B. Power, © 1999. Portsmouth, NH: Heinemann.

"Big Ideas" in Science

Most of us have a few strong memories of learning science in school. Some of the memories are funny or flamboyant—we might think of a classmate who designed a papier-mâché volcano exploding with fire and minimarshmallows for the science fair. Other memories might be downright painful, especially if you're the student who fainted while dissecting a frog in a high school lab.

Many of us equate science with the smell of formaldehyde or the recitation of specific facts. But science is so much more than experiments with beakers or complicated formulas. Young children have a natural curiosity about how the world works—at its most simple level, developing this curiosity is what science is all about. Parents and teachers can tap into that curiosity to explore some of the "big ideas" that will shape all their future work in science.

If you are interested in helping your child develop some basic skills and thinking in the area of science at home, you can talk about and reinforce the following concepts. By helping your child think about these "big ideas," you'll give them a head start in developing scientific awareness. And you won't be forced to construct a volcano out of papier-mâché or dissect a frog.

- **Cause and Effect**
The principle of "cause and effect" can be explored in any household—especially in the kitchen. Your child can learn that when you put water in the freezer, it hardens. When chocolate chips are heated on the stove, they melt. Any time you talk with your child about a change, pointing to a cause, you are helping them make the link between cause and effect.

- **Organization**
Throughout the natural world, there are classification systems. Well before children start mastering complicated hierarchies of plants and organisms, they can learn how different things in your house and yard are sorted, or sort themselves out. Looking at how ants organize themselves on the front yard, or how fish establish a pecking order in a tank, or how you keep books and videotapes sorted, teaches them about how essential organization and classification is in the world.

Support your child's natural wondering about how the world works, and you will promote a love of science.

Los principales conceptos científicos

La mayoría de nosotros tenemos recuerdos de cuando estudiamos ciencias en la escuela. Algunos de los recuerdos son cómicos. Por ejemplo, podemos tener el recuerdo de un compañero que haya presentado en la feria de ciencias un volcán diseñado con papel-mâché que podía hacer erupción y arrojar pequeñas alteas al aire. Otros recuerdos pueden ser francamente dolorosos, especialmente si usted es el estudiante que se desmayó mientras disecaba una rana cuando estaba en la escuela secundaria.

Muchos de nosotros asociamos la clase de ciencias con el mal olor del formaldehído o la memorización de datos específicos. Pero las ciencias son mucho más que experimentos con vasos de laboratorio o fórmulas complicadas. Los niños tienen una curiosidad natural acerca de cómo funciona el mundo. A su nivel más elemental, la ciencia trata precisamente de desarrollar esta curiosidad. Los padres y maestros pueden intervenir en esa curiosidad para explorar los " principales conceptos" que rigen las ciencias y que conformarán todo el trabajo de su hijo(a) en ese campo.

Si usted está interesado en ayudar a su hijo(a) a desarrollar algunas habilidades básicas y a pensar en las ciencias cuando está en casa, lo mejor es hablar de los siguientes conceptos y y reforzarlos. Al ayudar a su hijo(a) a pensar en los principales conceptos científicos, usted le dará un punto de partida intelectual para desarrollar el conocimiento científico. Y, por otra parte, usted no se verá en la obligación de hacer cosas tales como un volcán de papel maché o disectar una rana.

- **Causa y efecto.**
  El concepto de "causa y efecto" se puede explorar en cualquier casa, especialmente en la cocina. Su hijo(a) puede aprender que cuando usted pone agua en el congelador, la misma se solidifica. Cuando las barras de chocolate se calientan en la hornilla, se derriten. Cada vez que habla con su hijo(a) acerca de un cambio, y señala la causa, lo está ayudando a establecer un vínculo entre la causa y el efecto.
- **Clasificación.**
  A lo largo del mundo natural existen sistemas de clasificación. Mucho antes de que los niños comiencen a dominar jerarquías complicadas de plantas y organismos, ellos pueden aprender a clasificar o categorizar diferentes cosas en su casa y en el patio. Observar la forma en que se organizan las hormigas en el jardín, o la forma en que los peces establecen un orden para alimentarse en una pecera, o la forma en que usted clasifica los libros y las videocintas, les enseña lo esencial que resulta la organización y clasificación en el mundo.

Apoye la curiosidad natural que demuestra su hijo(a) por entender el mundo que lo rodea y así le inculcará el amor por el estudio de las ciencias.

 Parent Power by B. Power, © 1999. Portsmouth, NH: Heinemann.

Childhood Friends

We all want children to learn in elementary school—but much of the most important learning doesn't involve academic subjects at all. Parents and teachers all want children to learn how to make friends and how to be a good friend. This learning is essential for their well-being and their continued success in the school community and at home. There are many things you can do as a parent to help your child navigate the tricky seas of friendship:

- **Teach your child that manners really do matter.**
  Many studies confirm that kids who easily make and keep friends give appropriate and supportive response to others regularly, without prompting. That means parents and teachers need to prompt children to say "please," "thank you," and "excuse me" a lot, until it becomes a habit.
- **Talk about friends who are important to you.**
  By understanding how and why you value your friends, your children will come to see the value of working on friendships.
- **Show your child the work of friendship.**
  Write cards together, make phone calls, send small gifts, or talk about why you send over an extra batch of cookies to a neighbor. Your child will see what pleasure comes from giving to others.
- **Ask about your child's friends.**
  If your child has a best friend, or friends they mention regularly, make asking about the friend's day a regular question you ask when quizzing your child on how their day went. Make a point of knowing the hobbies, interests, and personality quirks of your child's closest friends. By showing you care about your child's friends, you show your child how they are part of a larger community.
- **Discuss what being a friend means.**
  As your child gets older, it makes sense to talk more about friendship in general. What makes a good friend? What friends should be avoided? The answers to these questions will shape your child's social life for years to come.

Amigos de la niñez

Todos queremos que los niños aprendan en la escuela, pero mucho del aprendizaje más importante no tiene nada que ver con los aspectos académicos. Todos los padres y maestros desean que los niños aprendan cómo tener buenos amigos y ser buen amigo también. Este aprendizaje es esencial para su bienestar y su éxito continuo en la escuela y en el hogar. Existen muchas cosas que puede hacer como padre para ayudar a su hijo(a) a navegar por los mares engañosos de la amistad:

- **Enseñe a su hijo(a) que los buenos modales sí importan.**
  Muchos estudios confirman que los niños que hacen y mantienen amistades con facilidad brindan sistemáticamente una respuesta adecuada y estimulante a los otros, sin que se les sugiera. Esto significa que los padres y maestros necesitan sugerir a los niños que digan "por favor", "gracias" y "perdone" muchas veces, hasta que se convierta en un hábito.
- **Hable de amigos que son importantes para usted.**
  Al comprender cómo y por qué usted valora a sus amigos, sus hijos(as) llegarán a ver el valor de cultivar amistades.
- **Muestre a su hijo(a) cómo se cultiva la amistad.**
  Escriban cartas juntos, hagan llamadas telefónicas, envíen pequeños regalos, o hablen acerca de por qué usted envía una caja de galletitas a un vecino. Su hijo(a) verá el placer que causa el acto de dar a otros.
- **Pregunte por los amigos de su hijo(a).**
  Si su hijo(a) tiene un mejor amigo, o amigos que menciona frecuentemente, una pregunta que usted debe hacer cuando interrogue a su hijo(a) sobre los sucesos del día es acerca de cómo pasó el día de su amigo. Insista en conocer los pasatiempos, intereses y peculiaridades de los amigos más íntimos de su hijo(a). Al mostrar interés por los amigos de su hijo(a), usted le demuestra que es parte de una comunidad mayor.
- **Conversen acerca del significado de la amistad.**
  A la vez que crece su hijo(a), es lógico hablar más acerca de la amistad en general. ¿Qué es lo que hace a un buen amigo? ¿Qué tipo de amigos se deben evitar? Las respuestas a estas preguntas conformarán la vida social de su hijo(a) en los años por venir.

On Vacation...But Not from Learning!

Vacation is all about relaxing, and reconnecting with those we love. Getting renewed and back in touch is what matters most when families spend time together. But there are still opportunities for learning, both before and after any vacation trip. Here are some stress-free ways to link learning and fun on family vacations:

- **Have your child write or call the local travel bureau.**
  Many state travel bureaus have toll-free numbers or Web sites, as well as addresses for seeking information. If you have your child help you in the search for travel materials, they will have more interest in the trip. Coach your child first before they call a toll-free number. You may also want to listen in on another phone extension to fill in the gaps in the conversation. But if you have your child solicit information and get the materials mailed in their name, they are more likely to want to learn more about the trip before traveling.
- **Schedule a museum visit.**
  Find out what the local area is most known for historically or culturally, and then schedule a visit. But keep the visit short, and be flexible about trying to do the visit on a day when the weather isn't cooperating with you.
- **Keep a travel scrapbook.**
  Purchase an inexpensive blank scrapbook, and then stock a small kit with crayons, glue, tape, and markers. Being able to paste in odd souvenirs (like a strange napkin from a restaurant, or an odd-shaped leaf from a nature walk) will increase a child's interest in the scrapbook. Try to balance writing, sketching, and glued-in artifacts. Beyond the academic gains, the scrapbook is a wonderful filler for time when a car or plane ride gets long, or the family is forced to wait at a restaurant.

De vacaciones…¡pero sin dejar de aprender!

Las vacaciones son el tiempo de relajarse y volverse a unir con los seres que amamos. Sentirse renovados y volver a encontrarse es lo que más importa a las familias cuando pasan el tiempo juntas. Pero aún hay oportunidades para aprender, tanto antes como después de cualquier viaje de vacaciones. Aquí le ofrecemos algunas formas libres de estrés para vincular el aprendizaje y la diversión durante las vacaciones familiares:

- **Pida a su hijo(a) que escriba o llame a la oficina de turismo local.**
  Muchas oficinas estatales de turismo tienen números telefónicos gratuitos o sitios en la Red, al igual que direcciones para buscar información. Si usted pide a su hijo(a) que lo ayude a buscar materiales turísticos, él tendrá más interés en el viaje. Instruya a su hijo(a) primero antes de que llame a un número gratuito. Usted tal vez quiera oír en otra extensión para llenar cualquier vacío que pudiera surgir en la conversación. Pero si hace que su hijo(a) solicite información y pida que le envíen los materiales por correo a su nombre, es más probable que se interese más en él antes de emprenderlo.
- **Programe una visita al museo.**
  Averigüe cuáles son los puntos más conocidos en su área por su interés cultural o histórico y planifique una visita. Pero haga que sea corta la misma y sea flexible en cuanto a tratar de hacer la visita en un día si el tiempo no lo favorece.
- **Conserve un álbum de recortes.**
  Compre un álbum de recortes en blanco que no sea caro, y prepare un pequeño juego de creyones, goma de pegar, cinta adhesiva y marcadores. El hábito de pegar recuerdos raros en el álbum (tales como una extraña servilleta de un restaurante, o una hoja de forma rara que hayan recogido durante un paseo por parajes naturales) aumentará el interés de su hijo(a) en el mismo. Trate de buscar un equilibrio entre escribir, dibujar y otras actividades manuales, como pegar. Más allá de lo que pueda contribuir al avance académico de su hijo(a), el álbum de recortes es un modo maravilloso de emplear el tiempo cuando un viaje por carro o por avión se hace muy largo, o cuando la familia se ve obligada a esperar mucho tiempo en un restaurante.

Spelling

Imagine trying to learn to ride a bike without ever falling off or learning to play the piano without ever hitting a wrong note. It can't be done—learning to do anything well involves taking risks and making mistakes. Learning to spell is also a process of trial and error in schools and at home.

Parents of young children are understandably concerned when they see writing with spelling errors. It's important to see these errors in the context of how they are used to understand and instruct your child. Teachers often call the misspellings of young children "invented," "temporary," or "phonetic" spelling to express that misspellings are merely a stage in development—a necessary, temporary step in the path toward conventional spelling. Here's what you can do to help your child with spelling:

- **Look at percentages of correctly spelled words.**
  Many young children will know how to spell less than a dozen words correctly in the first year or two of school. Though their writing may still have many errors in the first or second grade, you should be able to see steady progress in the amount of words that are spelled correctly.
- **Read and write at home.**
  Research shows that the single greatest way to help your child develop ability as a speller is to expose them to more words in a stress-free environment. Reading together at home for fun, and providing opportunities to write lists and short letters, gives your child opportunities to practice and develop skills as a writer.
- **Ask about spelling in school.**
  There are times when correct spelling is essential, and there are other times when early drafts of materials will include many misspelled words. Your child's teacher can explain the reasoning beyond the spelling component of their reading and writing program.
- **Don't focus on correct spelling too much.**
  Just handling a pencil is a very hard task in terms of hand-eye coordination for young children. If everything they write is viewed as "wrong," they will soon see writing as drudgery, or a task that dooms them to failure. If you overlook misspelled words, you might be surprised at how much writing your children does—and how many more correctly spelled words quickly begin to emerge in their writing.

Learning to play the piano or ride a bike can be very difficult—so can learning to spell for young children. But with patience, you and your child will see progress over time. And when your child is all grown up and spells beautifully, you will probably look back with nostalgia at some of their early misspellings. These errors won't last forever, and they mark a time when learning to write is new and exciting for your child.

La ortografía

Imagínese lo difícil que sería aprender a montar en bicicleta sin caerse nunca o aprender a tocar el piano sin haber tocado nunca una nota equivocada. No es posible. El aprender a hacer algo bien implica asumir riesgos y cometer errores. Aprender la ortografía es también un proceso de ensayos y errores en la escuela y en el hogar.

Es comprensible que los padres de niños pequeños se preocupen cuando los ven escribir con errores de ortografía. Es importante ver esos errores en el contexto de cómo se usan para entender e instruir a su hijo(a). A veces los maestros llaman a esas faltas de ortografía que cometen los niños "grafías inventadas", "grafías temporales", o bien, ortografía "fonética" para expresar que las mismas son sólo una etapa en el desarrollo, es decir, un paso necesario y temporal en el camino hacia la ortografía convencional. A continuación verá lo que puede hacer para ayudar a su hijo(a) con la ortografía:

- **Fíjese en el porcentaje de palabras escritas correctamente.**
  Muchos niños pequeños sabrán cómo escribir correctamente menos de una docena de palabras en el primer o segundo año escolar. Aunque su escritura pueda tener aún muchos errores en primer o segundo grado, usted debe estar en condiciones de ver un progreso sostenido en la cantidad de palabras que su hijo(a) escribe correctamente.
- **Leer y escribir en la casa.**
  Las investigaciones revelan que la mejor forma de ayudar a su hijo(a) a desarrollar habilidades ortográficas es hacer que se enfrente a un mayor número de palabras en un medio libre de estrés. Leer juntos en la casa como entretenimiento y proporcionar ocasiones de escribir listas y cartas cortas, le da a su hijo(a) oportunidades de practicar y desarrollar habilidades como escritor.
- **Averigüe qué lugar ocupa la ortografía en la escuela.**
  Hay momentos en que resulta esencial la ortografía, y hay otros en que los primeros borradores de algunos materiales tendrán muchas palabras mal escritas. El maestro de su hijo(a) puede explicar el razonamiento más allá del componente ortográfico de su programa de lectura y escritura.
- **No se concentre demasiado en la ortografía correcta.**
  Para los niños pequeños, el solo hecho de tomar un lápiz es una tarea muy difícil en términos de la coordinación necesaria entre la vista y la mano. Si usted le hace creer que todo lo que escribe está "incorrecto", su hijo(a) pronto verá la escritura como una faena penosa, o una tarea que los lleva al fracaso. Si usted pasa por alto las palabras mal escritas, podrá sorprenderse de lo mucho que escriben sus hijos(as) y cuántas más palabras correctamente escritas empiezan a surgir en su escritura.

Aprender a tocar el piano o a montar en bicicleta puede ser muy difícil, igual que puede ser difícil para un niño pequeño aprender a escribir correctamente. Pero con paciencia, usted y su hijo(a) verán progresos con el tiempo. Y cuando su hijo(a) haya crecido y escriba perfectamente, probablemente usted recuerde con nostalgia algunos de sus primeros errores de ortografía. Esos errores no durarán siempre, y marcan una etapa en la cual aprender a escribir es nuevo y emocionante para su hijo(a).

   Parent Power by B. Power, © 1999. Portsmouth, NH: Heinemann.

A Love of Music

Long before that dancing baby in cyberspace captured everyone's attention, we learned that children love music. All anyone has to do to see how deep this love runs is to watch children at a concert. Put on any music with a lively beat, and it's almost impossible to stop a young child from shaking, shimmying, and clapping their hands.

Beyond the pleasure of listening to music, nurturing your child's love of music can help develop many skills necessary for success in life. Research links music and math abilities. The process of playing an instrument also fosters growth in hand-eye coordination, and the ability to concentrate for longer periods of time.

Helping your child appreciate music doesn't have to be time-consuming or expensive. Because we are surrounded by music in the home, in the car, and at retail shops, it's easy to focus with your child on the rhythms around us:

- **Help your child notice the emotional aspect of the music.**
  Ask, "What music makes you happy? What music makes you sad? Why?"
- **Clap along.**
  As simple as it sounds, clapping tunes a child into the song, links the melody to a beat, and helps children develop a sense of rhythm.
- **Attend free concerts.**
  There are often concerts available for free at local high schools, as well as summertime festivals in parks and at the mall.

If you do think your child is ready for music lessons, get a little advice before you take the plunge. Think about whether or not your child would enjoy individual or group lessons—different personalities will work best with different options. Talk to a local music teacher about what musical instruments are easiest for young children to begin on, and check at a local music store or with a school music teacher to see about the possibility of renting first, or buying used equipment.

Before you know it, you and your child will be building memories of favorite and least favorite songs together. And it's good to build those memories while your child is young—parents of teenagers will tell you that sharing the same musical tastes with your child may not last forever!

El amor por la música

Mucho antes de que un bebé que baila en el ciberespacio captara la atención de todos, aprendimos que a los niños les gusta la música. Todo lo que tiene que hacer cualquiera para ver hasta qué punto les gusta es observar a los niños en un concierto. Ponga una música con un ritmo alegre y es casi imposible impedir a un niño pequeño que se mueva, dé vueltas y palmadas.

Más allá del placer de escuchar la música, fomentar en su hijo el amor por la música puede ayudar a desarrollar muchas habilidades necesarias para el éxito en la vida. Las investigaciones vinculan la música con las habilidades matemáticas. El proceso de tocar un instrumento también favorece el desarrollo de la coordinación entre la vista y la mano y la capacidad de concentrarse por largos períodos de tiempo.

Ayudar a que su hijo(a) aprecie la música no tiene que ser una actividad cara o a la que hay que dedicar mucho tiempo. Ya que estamos rodeados de música en la casa, en el carro y en las tiendas, resulta fácil enfocar la atención suya y la de su hijo(a) en los ritmos que nos rodean:

- **Ayude a su hijo(a) a notar el aspecto emocional de la música.**
  Pregunte: "¿Qué tipo de música te hace feliz? ¿Qué tipo de música te pone triste? ¿Por qué?"
- **Dé palmadas.**
  Tan simple como suena, acompañar las canciones con palmadas ayuda a su hijo a captar el ritmo de la melodía, lo cual ayuda a su hijo(a) a desarrollar el sentido del ritmo en general.
- **Asista a conciertos gratis.**
  A veces en las escuelas secundarias hay conciertos gratis, al igual que festivales de verano en parques y en centros comerciales.

Si piensa que su hijo(a) está preparado para tomar clases de música, pida consejos antes de que se decida. Piense si su hijo(a) disfrutará de las clases individuales o en grupo. Cada tipo de personalidad se desenvuelve mejor con éstas o aquellas opciones. Hable con un maestro de música local acerca de qué instrumentos musicales son más fáciles para que los niños empiecen con ellos y visite la tienda de música local o consulte con un maestro de música de la escuela la posibilidad de alquilarlos primero, o de comprar instrumentos usados.

Antes de darse cuenta, usted y su hijo(a) estarán creando recuerdos juntos de las canciones favoritas. Y es bueno ir creando esos recuerdos de cuando su hijo(a) era pequeño. Los padres de adolescentes le dirán que la posibilidad de compartir con su hijo(a) los mismos gustos musicales no es algo que durará para siempre.

Telling Family Tales

Children loving hearing stories of when their parents or grandparents were young. Sharing family tales and traditions inspires children and makes them feel more secure as part of a large, extended network. There are big and small ways to help your child understand the heritage of your family:

- **Cook and talk about recipes passed down in family.**
  This will build your child's sense of your family's ethnic history, as well as the special tastes and meals enjoyed by family members for generations.
- **Use a map to give children a sense of place as you share family stories.**
  If your family emigrated from another country, or even has moved around quite a bit within the country or state, use a map to show different locations. Even a young child gains a sense of perspective in distance when you show the route traveled from overseas to the United States, as compared to moving from city to city within your state.
- **Talk about family physical characteristics.**
  Children love the novelty of learning that every member of one side of the family has an especially long third toe. By pointing out distinctive birthmarks or an eye color that passes from generation to generation, you help your child get a rudimentary awareness of genetics.
- **Pull out those black sheep!**
  Of course, you won't want to share the raciest tidbits of your family's history with a young child. But children are delighted to hear about the more eccentric branches of the family tree. If a favorite aunt of yours always used her teabags at least six times, you might talk about the frugality inspired by the Great Depression. This might in turn lead to discussions of the value of recycling and frugality today. But don't force the academic connections. There may be little new learning involved when you tell the story of a prankster cousin who enjoyed cracking raw eggs on his sister's head—but you'll definitely share some good giggling over the tale.

When children learn about how far past generations of their family have traveled, the adversity they overcame, and the unique personality quirks passed down through the family, they gain confidence. They know they are part of a special group of people, sharing a love borne of experiences and traditions carried through many generations.

   Parent Power by B. Power, © 1999. Portsmouth, NH: Heinemann.

Cuentos de la familia

A los niños les gusta oír cuentos de cuando sus padres o abuelos eran pequeños. Compartir las historias y tradiciones familiares inspira a los niños y los hace sentirse más seguros como parte de una red grande y extensa. Hay formas sencillas y complicadas de ayudar a que su hijo(a) entienda el legado de su familia:

- **Cocine y hable sobre recetas que se han heredado de la familia.**
  Esto dará a su hijo(a) un sentido de la herencia étnica de su familia, al igual que le permitirá disfrutar los sabores especiales de que han disfrutado los miembros de la familia por generaciones.
- **Use un mapa para dar a los niños un sentido de lugar al compartir historias de la familia.**
  Si su familia emigró de otro país o si se ha mudado varias veces dentro del país o estado, use un mapa para mostrar los diferentes lugares. Hasta un niño pequeño adquiere un sentido de la distancia cuando usted muestra la ruta que siguió cuando viajó del extranjero a los Estados Unidos, en comparación con mudarse de una ciudad a otra dentro de su estado.
- **Hable acerca de las características físicas de la familia.**
  A los niños les encanta la novedad de conocer que cada miembro de una parte de la familia tiene el tercer dedo del pie particularmente largo. Al señalar rasgos de nacimiento característicos en el color de los ojos que pasan de una generación a otra, usted ayuda a su hijo(a) a adquirir un conocimiento rudimentario de genética.
- **¡Saque esa oveja negra!**
  Por supuesto, usted no querrá compartir las anécdotas más picantes de la historia de su familia con un niño pequeño. Pero a los niños les encanta oír cosas sobre las ramas más excéntricas de su árbol familiar. Si su tía favorita siempre usaba sus bolsitas de té al menos seis veces, usted puede hablar de la frugalidad que inspiró la Gran Depresión. Esto puede a su vez llevar a conversaciones sobre el valor del reciclaje y la frugalidad en nuestros días. Pero no fuerce los vínculos con asuntos académicos. Puede parecer que no se aprende nada nuevo cuando usted cuenta la historia de un primo bromista a quien le gustaba romper huevos crudos en la cabeza de su hermana, pero de seguro provocará algunas risas con el cuento.

Cuando los niños conocen de qué lugares tan lejanos han viajado las pasadas generaciones de su familia, las adversidades por las que han atravesado y las peculiaridades de la personalidad que se han transmitido a través de la familia, se sienten más seguros de sí mismos. Los niños saben que pertenecen a un grupo especial de personas, que comparten un amor nacido de experiencias y tradiciones mantenidas por muchas generaciones.

   Parent Power by B. Power, © 1999. Portsmouth, NH: Heinemann.

Stress and Learning

Growing up is hard work! Young children have a lot to sort through—making new friends, peer rules on the playground, letters and numbers that must be understood for success in the classroom. No wonder most children occasionally exhibit some signs of stress in the early years of school. As a parent, you can look for the symptoms of stress and take some simple steps to help your child cope with daily problems as they come up.

Signs of stress include a child who becomes more fearful, clingy, or far more quiet than usual. Changes in eating patterns also point to stress (either not eating enough or consuming far more food than normal). Often problems at night are the first signal—stressed-out kids will have trouble getting to sleep or wake up often in the night. They may experience frequent nightmares, or even return to bedwetting.

So what can parents do to help children deal with stress? At the root of stress is a feeling of not having enough control—both of events and of emotions. The goal is to help children learn how to solve problems daily and master their emotions, without fleeing from what's bothering them or always turning to adults for help. As a parent, you can:

- **Provide regular routines.**
  Bedtime routines are especially important; they give children a sense that there are activities and rituals (bath, books, talk) that always take place, no matter what goes wrong in the day.
- **Listen and validate your child's concerns.**
  Don't dismiss any problem as trivial. Ask, "Why does that bother you?" "What could you do to change the situation?" Just by identifying the stress, you'll help your child feel more in control.
- **Ensure daily down time.**
  Everyone needs quiet time to relax their minds. Make sure there is at least some time every day when the television and stereo are off—you will be surprised at how calming the effect is for everyone.

Perhaps the most important remedy for stress is preventive. Ask you child daily if they had a good day or a bad day. Sorting through with them what makes days good and bad gives them a sense of their needs and power.

Estrés y aprendizaje

¡Crecer es una tarea ardua! Los niños pequeños tienen que enfrentar muchas cosas: nuevas amistades, reglas de compañerismo en el parque o patio de recreo, letras y números que se deben aprender para tener éxito en la clase. No es de extrañar que la mayoría de los niños muestren ocasionalmente algunos signos de estrés en los primeros años escolares. Como padre, usted puede buscar los síntomas del estrés y dar algunos pasos simples para ayudar a su hijo(a) a enfrentar los problemas diarios cuando surjan.

Los signos del estrés incluyen que un niño se vuelva más temeroso, más apegado o mucho más tranquilo de lo usual. El cambio en los hábitos alimenticios apunta también hacia el estrés (bien sea no comer lo suficiente o consumir mucha más comida de lo normal). Muchas veces, la primera señal son los problemas por la noche. Los niños con estrés tienen dificultad en quedarse dormidos o se despiertan con frecuencia durante la noche. Pueden tener pesadillas frecuentes o hasta volver a orinarse en la cama.

¿Qué pueden hacer los padres para ayudar a los niños a enfrentar el estrés? En el fondo, el estrés es el resultado de sentir que uno no tiene suficiente control, tanto de los eventos como de las emociones. El objetivo es ayudar a los niños a que aprendan a solucionar los problemas diariamente y a que controlen sus emociones, sin huir de aquello que les molesta ni recurrir siempre a los adultos en busca de ayuda. Como padre, usted puede:

- **Proporcionar rutinas estables.**
  Las rutinas en cuanto a la hora de acostarse son especialmente importantes. Estas rutinas dan a los niños un sentido de que hay actividades y rituales (el baño, los libros, la conversación) que siempre tienen lugar, sin importar lo que no haya marchado bien durante el día.
- **Escuchar y confirmar las preocupaciones de su hijo(a).**
  No descarte ningún problema como algo sin importancia. Pregunte, "¿Por qué eso te molesta?" "¿Qué puedes hacer para cambiar la situación?" Sólo con identificar el estrés, ayudará a su hijo a sentirse en mayor control de la situación.
- **Reserve un tiempo de calma todos los días.**
  Todo el mundo necesita un tiempo de calma para relajar la mente. Asegúrese de disponer de algún tiempo cada día en que estén apagados el televisor y el equipo estereofónico. Usted se sorprenderá de la calma que produce esto en todo el mundo.

Tal vez el remedio más importante para el estrés es preventivo. Pregunte a su hijo(a) diariamente si ha tenido un buen o mal día. Al examinar con su hijo(a) los elementos que hacen que un día resulte bueno o malo los hará más conscientes de sus necesidades y les dará un buen sentido de poder.

 Parent Power by B. Power, © 1999. Portsmouth, NH: Heinemann.